LIGHTFOOT WINDS

The Capture of Guadeloupe
by the British in 1815.

By the same author

THE LIFE OF SIR JOHN FORBES

LIGHTFOOT WINDS

The Capture of Guadeloupe
by the British in 1815.

DR. ROBIN A. L. AGNEW
Emeritus Consultant Chest Physician, Liverpool

Bernard Durnford Publishing

LIGHTFOOT WINDS
The Capture of Guadeloupe
by the British in 1815.

First published by Bernard Durnford Publishing 2005
This impression in a larger format with additions 2019
by Bernard Durnford Publishing

A catalogue record of this book
is available from the British Library

ISBN 978-1-904470-16-8
Format, design and cover by StewART

DEDICATION:

TO MY GRANDCHILDREN -

Timothy, Eleanor, Adam,
Jack, Molly and Tilly

Lightfoot Winds

CONTENTS

LIST OF ILLUSTRATIONS

Figure 1)   Mersey Docks and Harbour Board Building.
Page 25   Completed in 1907.
(Original in LIVERPOOL - *City of
Architecture* by Quentin Hughes.
The Bluecoat Press, Liverpool.
Second edition, 1999; p 131.)

Figure 2)   *The Battlefield of Ballinamuck* by unknown
Page 27   artist. (Courtesy of John Rylands University
Library, Manchester.)

Figure 3)   Portrait of Dr John Forbes as a Physician at
Page 31   Chichester. Painted by a local artist, James
Andrews. With acknowledgements to the
Postgraduate Medical Centre,
St Richard's Hospital, Chichester.
Reproduced by kind permission of the Editor,
Journal of Medical Biography.
(*J Med Biog* 1994, 2: 187-192).

Figure 11) Tapestry fire-screen showing Sir John's
Page 60 coat of arms and motto *Labore*
Robore Spe (By Work, Strength, Hope);
by kind permission of Mr David
Forbes FRCS, FRACS of Burradoo,
New South Wales and the Forbes
family in Australia.

Figure 12) James Johnson (1777-1845). Lithograph by
Page 63 T Brigford. R Burgess: Portraits of Doctors
and Scientists, The Wellcome Institute,
London 1973, No.1538.3.
Courtesy of the Wellcome Institute Library,
London.

Figure 13) Admiral Charles Middleton (1726-1813).
Page 65 British School 19c. Courtesy
National Maritime Museum.

Figure 18) Memorial plaque of Sir John Forbes in
Page 124 Whitchurch Parish Church with
            acknowledgements to the Rector,
            the Rev. R. Hughes. Reproduced
            by kind permission of The Editor,
            Journal of Medical Biography.
            (*J Med Biog* 1996; 4: 178-183)

ACKNOWLEDGEMENTS:

It gives me great pleasure to acknowledge the help that I have received from many individuals and organisations. Firstly, Mr Graham Salt, Research Historian of Fareham, spent many hours at the National Archives in Kew, which resulted in a complete record of Forbes' naval service. As may be seen in the text, I have relied heavily on this research compiled from entries in Captain's/Master's Logs (ADM 51/- & ADM 52/-). The dates of arrival and departure are also taken from the Ship's Muster Books (ADM 37/-). Without this information, I should have been unable to write this book.

Surgeon Commodore N.E. Baldock QHP, Royal Navy authorised the reproduction of the figures previously published in my article *Fortune favours the Brave - The Capture of Guadeloupe 1815*, which appeared in the Journal of the Royal Naval Medical Service (1997) 82: 2, pp 94-98.

Sir James Watt KBE, formerly Medical Director General (Naval) 1972-77, has helped me with references and particularly with regards to scurvy in the Royal Navy, a subject on which he is a leading authority.

I am grateful to Mrs J.V.S. Wickenden of the Historic Collections

Library at the Institute of Naval Medicine,Gosport for valuable information on the staff and their annual wages at Haslar in early 1811; also for her review (*J Royal Naval Medical Service* 2003,Vol. 89.2, 96-7) of my biography of Sir John Forbes (1787-1861).

The map of the Caribbean, showing the island of Guadeloupe is reproduced by kind permission of Euan Macnaughton Associates, Syndication Agents for The Telegraph plc.

Permission to reproduce the picture of Admiral Durham is gratefully acknowledged to Bonhams, Scotland.

For valuable information on the Parish School at Fordyce and the *George Smith Bursary* together with photographs of the headstones in the 'Auld Kirkyard' and for a map of Banffshire, I am indebted to Mrs Christine Urquhart of Fordyce.

The quotation on page 124 is taken from the poem 'Into Battle' by Julian Grenfell in The little book of War poems, edited by Nick De Somogyi, published by Marks and Spencer plc 2001, created by Magpie Books, an imprint of Constable & Robinson Ltd. Permission to quote this verse has been kindly given by the Book Department of Marks and Spencer. Julian Henry Francis Grenfell (1888-1915), who was educated at Eton and Balliol

ACKNOWLEDGEMENTS Continued:

College, was an English poet. He was mortally wounded at Ypres and died in hospital at Boulogne in May 1915. He is remembered for his war poem 'Into Battle', which was published in The Times in 1915.

Mrs A Wareham, Librarian and Head of Information Services at the Royal Naval Museum, Portsmouth gave me an important reference about the use of carronades in the Royal Navy. Mr David Taylor and his staff at the Picture Library of the National Maritime Museum, Greenwich have also been very helpful in supplying photographs for illustrations.

I am grateful to Mrs Eleanor Sharpston QC for her comments on the whereabouts of the capture of the French 'Seventy-Four' D'Hautpolt. (Ref.68). The Sailing Navy List (1993), by her late husband Mr David Lyon, was an invaluable source of information on the ships of the Royal Navy, built, purchased or captured between 1688 and 1855.

I should also like to thank Dr D. Geraint James FRCP for writing the Foreword to my book and for his constructive criticism of my original text.

Brian Lavery's Nelson's Navy has been a major fund of knowledge to me as shown by the frequency it is quoted in the list of references. As the late Patrick O'Brian CBE wrote in his Foreword to that work: '...there is no royal road to a knowledge of the navy of Nelson's time...but Brian Lavery's Nelson's Navy is the most regal that I have come across in many years of reading on the subject'.

Fiona Cooney of Longford County Library and Arts Services has provided me with much helpful information on Castle Forbes and Newtownforbes, Co. Longford and I am truly grateful. In particular the article on Castle Forbes by James Fleming was invaluable.

The staff at the John Rylands University Library at Manchester went to a lot of trouble in finding the picture of The Battlefield of Ballinamuck in History of the County Longford by JP Farrell for me.

I am also indebted to Miss S.G. Williams for word processor and computer advice and to all the staff at Ormskirk Public Library for help with tracing references.

To all these in general, and to many whose names are not mentioned, I am deeply appreciative; in particular, for the forbearance of my wife, Ann, during the time that I have devoted to 'Forbes' and for her helpful criticism and advice.

ACKNOWLEDGEMENTS Continued:

Our very best efforts have been made to obtain copyright permission for each illustration but if any copyright owner has been overlooked, please inform the Publisher. I should like especially to acknowledge the help of the late Bernard Durnford and - more recently - that of Stewart Antill and Barry Hughes, Stewart, in particular, has been brilliant!

I very much appreciate the detailed information about Dr David McBride (1726-78), which was obtained from Dr Edward Martin's major work on ...*Bookplates of Irish Medical Doctors, with short biographies.* This contribution to Irish medical history has been very well received both in Dublin and in London.

A late addition to my source of references was Professor N.A.M. Rodger's magnificent Naval History of Britain, 1649-1815, published in 2004. It is not only well written but it contains a mine of information on how this country gained *The Command of the Ocean,* which lasted for nearly the ensuing century. There is also a valuable *English Glossary* at the back of the book, which explains, in alphabetical order, nautical terminology ranging from *aback* to *yawl.*

Finally, I apologise for any solecisms in the text. For instance, I have spelt the possessive of the family name of Forbes with the apostrophe following the final 's'.

Foreword
by Dr. D. Geraint James
Former Consultant Physician to the Royal Navy

Britain is celebrating the bicentenary of the Battle of Trafalgar in 2005, so we are gloomily reliving the last hours of the life of Admiral Lord Nelson in Victory, but also stirred by an epic triumph involving, amongst others, Admiral Cuthbert Collingwood in the Royal Sovereign and Captain Eliab Harvey in Temeraire. At that time John Forbes was a student at the University of Aberdeen and – no doubt inspired by Nelson's victory at Trafalgar – he decided to enlist in the Navy. He entered in the rank of temporary assistant surgeon following tuition in Edinburgh and a diploma of the Royal College of Surgeons. This scholarly biography, Lightfoot Winds, outlines his childhood, naval career (1807 – 1816), medical practice in Chichester (1822 – 1840), medical journalism and other claims to fame. Forbes was a prolific letter-writer to his contemporaries, who included Sir Walter Scott, Charles Dickens, Florence Nightingale and Sir Robert Peel. What a background for a biography or even, surely, a film to remember. After reading this book, consider the actors who could possibly fulfil the film roles of Forbes and the other characters.

Robin Agnew has moulded all these many different lives of Sir John Forbes – Royal Physician, translator of Laënnec, Victorian polymath and Fellow of the Royal Society (1829) into a fascinating and lively tale set in the nineteenth century. Readers will surely enjoy and suffer my emotions: I just could not put it down until I had completed it. You will no doubt also feel that it is the perfect companion for a long and otherwise boring air journey.

From the fulsome well-directed acknowledgements it is evident that the author has reached a rich seam at the coalface of information relating to Sir John Forbes; not only facts but also with eighteen illustrations of portraits and naval scenes. It has also been a pleasure handling this book not only because of the reading matter but also because the publishers, Bernard Durnford Publishing, have made it easy to view and to handle.

D. Geraint James
London, August 2005.

PROLOGUE:

THE NAVAL HYMN
Eternal Father, strong to save,
Whose arm doth bind the restless wave,
Who bidd'st the mighty ocean deep
Its own appointed limits keep:
O hear us when we cry to thee
For those in peril on the sea.[1]

The first verse of the naval hymn sums up the spiritual feelings of many of those who "go down to the sea in ships: and do business in the great waters; these see the works of the Lord, and his wonders in the deep": these words from Psalm 107 are inscribed inside the first floor of the circular dome of the Mersey Docks and Harbour Board Building. Although we now live in more secular times, it is still appropriate to recall them in the context of John Forbes' naval career (1807-15) during the Napoleonic wars.

This building, [Fig.1] in addition to those of the Royal Liver and Cunard companies, completes the impressive waterfront known locally as the 'Three Graces'. Together they form a splendid architectural introduction to the Port of Liverpool.

The year 2003 was the 60th anniversary of the Battle of the Atlantic defeat of the U-Boat menace in WW II; the Liverpool skyline must have seemed a welcome sight to all those returning home safely from the storms and perils of North Atlantic convoys, even if some ships were still sunk by magnetic mines dropped in the river Mersey by the Luftwaffe!

The period of the later Napoleonic wars coincided with the time that the Royal Navy reigned supreme in its command of the seas following Admiral Viscount Nelson's (1758-1805) decisive victory over the combined fleets of France and Spain off Cape Trafalgar on the 21st October 1805. This triumph removed the threat of invasion by Napoleon's Grande Armée, which had just defeated the Austrians at Ulm; also of a repetition of the landing of a French army in Ireland: such an event had taken place at the time of an Irish nationalist uprising in 1798, which only ended with the surrender of a French force to the British at Ballinamuck, Co. Longford, on 8th September of that year[2]. [Fig.2]

Figure 1) Mersea Docks and Harbour Board Building
Completed in 1907.

The Bluecoat Press

Later minor reverses occurred during the war with the United States between 1812 and 1815, when the 'Yankees' scored some victories over the 'Limeys' in single ship frigate encounters in the North and South Atlantic, culminating in the action between the USS CHESAPEAKE and HMS SHANNON on the 1st June 1813. Captain Philip Broke won a decisive victory over Captain James Lawrence, who was mortally wounded as his frigate was outgunned by the Royal Navy'. (See *'The Command of the Ocean'* by NAM Rodger, (2004), 2, 1649-1815, 36; p.568).

John Forbes was not involved in any of these, although he did take part in some earlier naval actions in the Caribbean. These are documented engagements and, for their descriptions, I have relied upon the accounts written in the logs of the warships in which he served.

They are not as important in naval history as the deeds of such legendary heroes as Lord Nelson or Admiral Thomas Cochrane (1775-1860); nevertheless, they are worth recording as a tribute to a Scottish naval surgeon in the early nineteenth century. The following narrative of John Forbes' (later Sir John, 1853) adventures in the Royal Navy demonstrates clearly how they influenced his subsequent peacetime career as a Consulting Royal Physician and Medical Journalist; [Fig.3] but, first, we must consider his relatively humble beginnings in rural Scotland.

Figure 2) *The Battlefield of Ballinimuck* by unknown artist

John Rylands University Library

CHAPTER 1:
EARLY LIFE and EDUCATION

John Forbes was born on 17 December 1787 at Cuttlebrae in Rathven parish, Banffshire, Scotland. This lies inland near the mouth of the river Spey on the south coast of the Moray Firth, about sixty miles east of Inverness. He was the fourth son of Alexander Forbes (1750-1842), a local tenant farmer and Cicilia Wilkie (1752-1831). [3,4] In 1789 the family moved to a farm at Dytac (or Dytach) in the parish of Fordyce, a few miles away to the East. This was within easy reach of the coast at Sandend Bay, where young John learned to swim.

He attended the parish school at Fordyce, which later became Fordyce Academy in 1845-46. The local schoolmaster was Alexander Gray but he left to take up farming in 1801. This was in the year that William Cruickshank, an MA of King's College, Aberdeen was appointed to succeed Gray; he remained at Fordyce until his death in 1854, aged 74. Academic standards improved under Cruickshank, who received an additional salary for tutoring boys for the *George Smith Bursary*. This was funded from a legacy donated by an ancestor of John Forbes' mother; a condition was that the bursary should be held by one of the founder's kin aged from eight to fourteen years. [5] As he left school at Fordyce in 1802 and would have reached the age of fifteen on 17 December of that year, Forbes may have qualified for the award of £25 pa. There is no doubt that he was well instructed in English composition, Latin and Greek grammar, and the French and Dutch languages.[6]

Cruickshank had been professor of mathematics at Aberdeen and was paid £40 pa salary as tutor for the 'Bounty boys'.[7] John would have had a good grounding in basic arithmetic, geometry, French, Latin and Greek; this was to prove vital in his subsequent career.

At this time, during their formative years at Fordyce, John Forbes met the young James Clark (1788-1870), who also came from farming stock. They became great friends and, in later life, their medical careers coincided. [Fig.4]

The original parish school at Fordyce dates back to the end of the 16th century; in 1679 a local benefactor, Walter Ogilvie, endowed the school with funds to provide an annual income for 20 children with education for five years at the school and for an additional 4 years of higher education at Aberdeen University. Both John Forbes and James Clark benefited from this *Bursary.*

In Fordyce churchyard there is a gravestone, which reads: 'Sacred to the memory of Alexander Forbes, formerly of Cuttlebrae in the parish of Ruthven, late of Dytach and Bogton in this parish, who departed this life on the 11th day of April 1842, aged 92 years; and of Cicilia Wilkie, his wife, who died on the 20th day of July 1831, in the 80th year of her age. Their bodies are here deposited and this stone is erected by their surviving children - Alexander, a merchant of Tepic in Mexico; John, physician in London; Elspet, and Anne, in commemoration of the work and virtues of most loving parents, and a lasting token of filial reverence, affection, and gratitude, A.D. 1843'. Just a few yards in front of the Forbes' plot, there is the gravestone of James Clark's parents, David Clark and Isabella Scott.

Young Forbes, aged 15, joined the Rector's class at Aberdeen Grammar School, where he expanded his knowledge of English, French and the Classics. From there he entered the Arts course of Marischal College at the University of Aberdeen in 1803. To attend, he tramped all the way on foot from his home at Dytac.

Figure 3) Portrait of Dr John Forbes as a Physician at Chichester.
Painted by a local artist, James Andrews.

Journal of Medical Biography

CHAPTER 2:
ENTRY AS 'TEMPORARY ASST.SURGEON'

John Forbes spent two years at Marischal College until 1805 but there is no record that he ever was rewarded with a BA degree from the University. He did, however, develop an interest in a future medical career and was apprenticed to two general practioners in the town of Banff.

At that time, an apprenticeship was the common form of entry into the medical profession, which was deeply divided between physicians and surgeons. The former were university graduates and had passed the examinations of the Royal College of Physicians. Surgeons were regarded more as tradesmen and were designated by the term "Mr" before their name although their craft may be traced back to prehistory, when flint tools had been used for draining abscesses and even for opening the skull by trepanning. [8] In the Middle Ages, operations were performed by 'barber-surgeons', hence the red and white striped pole over hairdressers' shops. In 1745, an Act of Parliament separated the Barbers of London from the Surgeons to incorporate a new Company of Surgeons, which became the Royal College of Surgeons in 1800 by Royal Charter.

In the early nineteenth century most common illnesses were dealt with by a low ranking class of general practitioner named an 'apothecary', who dispensed bottles and pills or by a 'surgeon-apothecary', if they opened abscesses etc. Diplomas were awarded to suitably experienced students, who satisfied the examiners of the Worshipful Society of Apothecaries in London. This was the route to qualification taken by the poet John Keats (1795-1821). [9]

In the autumn of 1805 Nelson's triumph at Trafalgar was universally acclaimed throughout the British Empire, especially in England, as the threat of a French invasion was removed at a stroke. As every schoolboy knows - or used to - this was achieved at the cost of the Admiral's life. Nelson's body, on board the *Victory*, was preserved in a cask of spirits and returned home to Spithead on 3rd December. Thence, with all honours, it was conveyed to the Painted Hall at Greenwich for the Lying-in-State from 4th to 5th January 1806. [Fig.5]

The final act has been vividly described: "On the 8th, in a violent south-west gale, the coffin was brought by river to the Admiralty in a long procession of State barges, attended by nine Admirals, five hundred Greenwich Pensioners, and the Lord Mayor and Corporation of London, and received at Whitehall Stairs by Norroy King of Arms, with nine heralds and pursuivants. On the 9th the funeral went in procession to St Paul's, where it may be said that England herself was visibly present". [10] There the navy was represented by Nelson's oldest friend, Sir Peter Parker (1721-1811), 30 Admirals, 100 Captains together with the Prince of Wales, representing King George III, and all the Royal Dukes. After an impressive choral funeral service, Garter King of Arms concluded his tribute to "the most Noble Lord Horatio Nelson..." with these words "...and the Hero who in the moment of Victory fell, covered with immortal glory!" [11] [Fig.6]

Figure 4) Portrait of Sir James Clark (1788-1870).

Wellcome Library, London

This may appear to be excessive to us; but there is no doubt that the victory at Trafalgar and Nelson's death reverberated around the British Isles in a spontaneous outburst of emotional catharsis. The fatal musket ball fired from the mizzen-top of the *Redoubtable* provoked a great wave of grief, mixed with affectionate admiration, for the little admiral in the land for which he gave his life.

During the year 1805, the 17-year-old John Forbes decided to enlist in the Royal Navy. He proceeded to Edinburgh and attended classes in medicine and surgery: he was awarded the Licentiateship of the Royal College of Surgeons of Edinburgh on 18 February 1806. [12] As the navy did not accept this qualification until 1826 but badly needed experienced surgeons, Forbes entered as a 'Temporary Asst. Surgeon' in January 1807 but was not entitled to call himself 'Surgeon' until his promotion to that rank on 27th January 1809, two years later. [13]

It is interesting to speculate on how the young Scot would have spent the time awaiting his 'call-up' papers. He may well have picked up a copy of James Lind's *On the Health of Seamen* (1762) in a second-hand bookshop in Edinburgh. James Lind (1716-1794), "the father of nautical medicine" is best known for his classical book on scurvy, which was first published in Edinburgh in 1753; a third edition appeared in 1772. Other books available to Forbes included: Observations on the Diseases Which Prevailed in H.M. Squadron in the Leeward Islands, published in 1800, by Dr Leonard Gillespie (1758-1842)[Fig.7] and On West India Diseases (1796) by Dr Benjamin Rush (1745-1813), an Edinburgh graduate. Rush was a renowned American physician from Philadelphia, who had signed the Declaration of Independence in 1776. He wrote on yellow fever epidemics, in which he advised bloodletting: for this he was criticized by Gillespie.

When the time came to join his ship at Devonport, Forbes decided to travel south by the cheapest means available.

According to Parkes, John Forbes "used to mention that he came up to London by a Leith smack, and was fourteen days on the passage, and that the journey to Plymouth to join the Royal George, to which ship he was appointed, took three days and nights more". [14] During his uncomfortable journey from the port of Edinburgh he would have had time to get used to the cramped living quarters in a fishing smack. The conditions on board would have served as a good introduction to life at sea in the Royal Navy!

Again, in order to save money, he would probably have travelled outside on top of the coach from London: three cold and cramped days and nights, with infrequent stops at inns en route to Devon.

Figure 5) Rear-Admiral Sir Horatio Nelson, 1758-1805)
by Lemuel Francis Abbott (1760-1803).

National Maritime Museum

CHAPTER 3:
MEDICAL QUALIFICATIONS FOR ENTRY

Owing to the shortage of properly qualified and experienced surgeons for the army and navy, the medical schools of Edinburgh and Dublin carried out 'crash programmes' in medicine and surgery for entry to the armed services. John Forbes had obtained the diploma of the College of Surgeons in 1806. In order to appreciate the significance of this, as regards the medical branch of the Royal Navy, we have to study the history of recognition by the Admiralty for the various degrees and diplomas that were available to students in the British Isles.

In 1629 the Company of Barber-Surgeons of London gained a monopoly of examining surgeons and surgeons' mates for the King's ships. In 1745 Parliament passed an Act making the Surgeons and the Barbers of London two separate and distinct corporations. The fledgling Company of Surgeons made sure that they retained the exclusive right to approve entrance to the Navy. Matters stayed the same until the end of the 18th century, when war broke out with Revolutionary France. At that time there was a shortage of medically qualified men for the naval service. One of the reasons for this was the high mortality in the Navy in the West Indies from yellow fever. Reluctantly, the Admiralty was forced to introduce new conditions in respect of 'surgical' appointments. In March 1797 the Royal College of Surgeons of Edinburgh, together with its sister college in Dublin, were approved by the Admiralty - but only in respect of surgeons' mates. Full surgeons were still only approved by the London Company.

During the 18th century, the Surgeons' Hall in London had maintained the sole right to examine candidates for the Army, the Honourable East India Company and the African slave trade.

In the second half of the 18th century trade rivalry with France developed into open warfare on the high seas, for which the East India Company raised large numbers of its own troops and also doctors. As the conditions on board their ships were good in comparison with the Royal Navy, they experienced no shortage of medical candidates.

It was very different in the African slave trade: this was a major business in the 18th century and, each year, many ships sailed from the ports of London, Bristol and Liverpool to the West African coast. (In 1771, it is said that Liverpool handled over 28,000 slaves and that, in the year that followed, more than 2,000 ships from Liverpool were involved in the trade). [17] This was known as the 'Guinea Trade' and many unfortunate slaves died on the infamous 'Middle Passage' between the African slave markets and the shores of the Caribbean and mainland America. The conditions in which the Negroes were kept below decks were indescribably squalid. Consequently, applications for surgeons' posts on the slave ships were few; those who did apply were often of little ability and with dubious qualifications.

Towards the end of the 18th century, public disapproval of the slave trade increased; the Government were forced to respond to the urgent pleas from such as James Ramsay (1733-1789), a retired naval surgeon and William Wilberforce (1759-1833). [18] Legislation made it compulsory for the owners of slave

Figure 6) The Death of Nelson painted in 1806
by Benjamin West (1738-1820).

Courtesy of Walker Art Gallery

ships to carry a surgeon, who had passed the qualifying examinations of the Surgeons' Hall in London.

By 1797 the strength of the Royal Navy had increased to
120,000 men. This required more surgeons in the Fleet but, as
demand exceeded supply, the Royal College in London
(founded in 1800) agreed to the Colleges of Surgeons in Edinburgh and Dublin in taking part in examinations for Surgeons'
mates. [19]

Act of Parliament finally abolished the British slave trade on
1st January 1808. About the same time the Edinburgh College
of Surgeons found a powerful ally in their bid to achieve parity
with the Royal College in London: he was Henry Dundas (1742-
1811), created Viscount Melville in 1802, who was First Lord of
the Admiralty in 1807. He pointed out forcefully that candidates
conferred with the Edinburgh diploma were instructed in both
medicine and surgery and were therefore qualified to act as
surgeons *and as physicians*. However, in spite of this argument,
the London College adamantly refused to recognise the Edinburgh surgical diploma until after the end of the war with
Napoleon in 1815. It was not until 1826 that the Edinburgh
College of Surgeons gained parity with the Colleges of London
and Dublin with regards to the appointment of *Surgeons* to the
Navy. This was extraordinary as, during the late eighteenth
century and the early part of the nineteenth century, students
flocked to the Edinburgh Medical School from all parts of the
British Isles as well as from overseas.

CHAPTER 4:
LIFE AFLOAT and NELSON'S TRADITION

John Forbes, after his lectures and practical demonstrations in anatomy and surgery at Edinburgh, would have been able to cope in an assistant capacity with most of the routine work in the 'sick berth'. He would have been helped by an unqualified assistant known as a 'loblolly boy'; the more complicated fractures and injuries would have come under the care of a 'full surgeon' in a Ship-of-the-Line such as the *Royal George*. (Being a three-decker, she would have had at least two other surgeons' mates). [20] He himself probably acted as a 'surgeon's mate', picking up knowledge of the navy and its ways, particularly in the care of the sick and injured, on a day-to-day basis.

It must be pointed out that a surgeon's status, both on shore and afloat, was lowly as operations were crude and limited - the only anaesthetic being a tot of rum. The young Scot would have become adept at suturing bleeding wounds and acting as surgeon, apothecary and physician all rolled into one! [21]The Surgeon lived in a cabin in the badly ventilated orlop deck but Forbes would have shared the midshipmen's' quarters on the lower deck. His 'action station' would have been the 'cockpit', where sea chests could be used as a crude operating table.

By this time, the cockpit was situated under the forecastle on the starboard side of the ship. The area, though cramped and only lit by a tallow candle, was protected from enemy musket fire; there the wounded were carried and treated "according to the time of their arrival in the cockpit, regardless of rank". [22]

What diseases would the young John Forbes have expected to see and treat? Venereal disease was very common in all navies and was accepted as part of the way of life of most seamen, especially after shore leave. However, up until the end of the eighteenth century the main disease to have plagued life at sea was scurvy.

In an epic voyage, lasting four years, Commodore George Anson (1697-1762) had circumnavigated the Globe but lost 1,400 of his men. [23] Of these, only four had been lost in battle, the main causes of death being scurvy and vitamin A and B deficiencies. [24] In 1747 the Scottish naval surgeon James Lind [Fig.8] conducted the first scrupulously controlled clinical trial on twelve seamen suffering from scurvy on board HMS *Salisbury*: he published his findings in his *Treatise of the Scurvy* in 1753. He clearly proved that the juice of oranges and lemons prevented the disease. Citrus fruits made up for the lack of Vitamin C in the usual ship's diet. Unfortunately, Lind did not have friends in high places at the Admiralty, so his advice was not acted upon. It was not until the mid-1790s that Ships' surgeons were issued with bottled lemon juice by the naval authorities, thus preventing the disease. [25]

Two other names of naval medical men should be mentioned for the parts they played in removing this blight from the Fleet, Gilbert Blane (1749-1834) and Thomas Trotter (1760-1832): both were Scots. Blane had a distinguished career in the navy and was later knighted for his efforts. Trotter, Physician to the Fleet (1794-1802), (see another view on p.88)

Figure 7) Leonard Gillespie, MD (1758-1842).

was also instrumental in making naval commanders aware of simple means of reducing sickness in their crews. Although lime-juice was never as effective as lemons in the treatment of scurvy, English ships earned the nickname of "limejuicers" and from mid-19th century the term "Limeys" came into use as a contemptuous expression for the British. [26]

The medical branch would also have been responsible for hygiene of the ship's company. Forbes would have attended cases of 'fever', for which the remedy was quinine in the form of 'Peruvian bark' of the cinchona tree dissolved in wine as a tincture to hide its bitter taste. Many cases of 'ship fever' were due to malaria or louse borne typhus but this was not recognised at the time. Amongst other diseases must be mentioned 'phthisis' or 'consumption', where the confined living quarters of the seamen provided the ideal environment for transmission of this infectious disease by coughing. There was no cure and the cause was not known until the discovery of the tubercle bacillus by the German pioneer bacteriologist Robert Koch (1843-1910) in 1882. Other common causes of disability were hernia, rheumatic disease and pneumonia. Alcoholism leading to persistent drunk-enness, especially if it occurred on duty, was punished by flogging with the cat-of-nine-tails, at which a surgeon would have to be present. [27]

During the course of an action at sea the cockpit was the scene of high drama: Nelson was wounded at Santa Cruz in the Canary Islands on the 25th July 1797, when he was 38 years of age. He was leading a landing party, with his customary bravery, on the mole of the harbour; under heavy fire from cannon and musketry, his right arm was shattered by grape shot. [28] The resulting operation in the cockpit of HMS Theseus was performed by lamplight with the ship rolling around in the waves and to the sound of the groans of the other wounded men. Nelson survived to fight another day at Trafalgar. Interestingly,

Figure 8) James Lind MD (1716-1794).
Physician of Haslar Hospital.

surgeon Thomas Eshelby was paid £36 for the operation, while his assistant, Louis Remonier, a 24 year old French Royalist serving in the Royal Navy with the rank of surgeon's mate received 24 guineas. [29] (The pay of a Full Surgeon was only about five pounds per month).

It must be said that John Forbes would not have been fully occupied for most of his time at sea, especially after his promotion to the rank of full surgeon. Then, he would have had spare time during a 'make and mend' to indulge in his passion for reading and studying foreign languages. He was probably happier at this time than at any other period in his life. These idyllic moments might be subject to interruption by such events as a cry of "man overboard", or a sailor falling from the top rigging onto the deck many feet below. If the unfortunate man survived, he might lie unconscious from a head injury with internal bleeding inside the skull. For this emergency some intrepid naval surgeons attempted the operation of trepanning: a small cylindrical disc was removed from the skull by using an instrument known as a trephine. In this way blood could be drained from beneath a depressed fracture of the skull with dramatic improvement in the patient's symptoms. For this the ship would have to be 'hove to' into the wind but even then, the surgeon needed to be extremely adroit to counteract the sea swell!

Such incidents have been described in the tales of the late Patrick O'Brian CBE, which are set in the Royal Navy during the Napoleonic wars. O'Brian based his novels on a sound knowledge of the naval history of the times. The following is an example of his style in describing surgeons' mates: "...wretched half grown stunted apprentices that have knocked about an apothecary's shop just long enough for the Navy Office to give them a warrant. They know nothing of surgery, let alone physic. They learn on the poor seamen as they go along, and they hope for an experienced loblolly boy or beast-leech or a cunning-man or maybe a butcher among the hands - the press brings in all sorts and when they have picked up a smattering of their trade, off they go into frigates or ships of the line". [30]

Although O'Brian was writing fictional tales of the sea, these words have the ring of truth about the kind of shipmates that Forbes would have met in his early days afloat. What they do not convey is the sense of the miserable conditions that seamen and, to a lesser extent their officers, had to cope with at sea. Often the victims of the notorious press gangs and without prior knowledge of the sea, they were expected to climb the rigging ratlines to the yardarms to manhandle the sails in all weathers; it was not surprising that some fell to their deaths. When there was a shortage of hands to man the ship, they would be expected to work 'watch and watch' with only four hours' sleep, cold and wet, in their hammocks slung above the crowded mess decks. Toileting and washing facilities were primitive and discipline harsh. Their only comfort was the daily issue of 'grog' (rum diluted with water), which was literally intended to "up spirits". Diet of salted meat and ship's biscuit was notoriously deficient in vitamin C but, in spite of all hardship, these were the men who fought their ships and guns (to which all deck space was sacrosanct) and won such victories for Nelson as 'St.Vincent' (1797), 'the Nile' (1798) 'Copenhagen (1801)' and 'Trafalgar' (1805).

Nelson's name is rightly revered in the Royal Navy but there was one curious incident in June 1799, which may have impugned his reputation. Following an insurrection at Naples, in which a Commodore Caracciola, a senior officer of the Neapolitan Navy, had been implicated and arrested, Nelson had him court-martialled. Caracciola was found guilty of treachery and, in spite of all pleas for clemency, was hanged from the yardarm of the Sicilian frigate *Minerva* on the orders of the

English admiral. For this summary execution of a flag officer of a foreign navy, Nelson has been criticised and it was rumoured that "the root cause of all the trouble was Lady Hamilton". [31] [Fig.9] 'In his defence it has been pointed out that Caracciolo of the Sicilian Navy was a deserter and had fired on a Sicilian frigate'. See Lambert A. In: *Nelson-Britannia's God of War* (2004), **IX**, p.158.

Whether or not her Ladyship was acting as a fin de siècle Salome is open to question but there seems no doubt that the precipitate action of the victor of 'the Nile' demonstrated an element of ruthlessness in his character. Lambert has devoted just over eight pages, with 33 references, in a scholarly discussion of the controversy. See Lambert A. *Nelson-Britannia's God of War*, (2004), appendix: 'The Black Legend', pp.365-373.

Was it just sheer bravado or a wish to die a noble death that induced him to appear on the deck of the *Victory*, exposed to the sharpshooters in the French mizzen tops? As he was already blind in one eye and starting to lose the sight in the other, it is tempting to speculate that he may have preferred a quick death in battle to becoming totally blind. The idea has been debunked by Dr A-M Hills in her book *Nelson – A Medical Casebook*, (2006), IX, pp.159 - 168, in which she makes a good case that suicide was totally opposed to Nelson's religious beliefs'. (See Further reading and Notes for Chapter 4).

It is very unlikely that these facets of Nelson's persona would have made a scrap of difference to young John Forbes at the time of joining his first ship in 1807. In fact many would remember the little admiral for his bravery in battle and his unique capacity for including his captains at *Trafalgar* in his overall strategy, at the same time leaving them to react independently in response to any tactical situation. This transcended any occasional foolhardiness and gave rise to the 'Nelson Touch', for which his memory is still cherished in the Royal Navy.

Figure 9) Lady Hamilton by Johann Schmidt
(1749-1828) in HMS *Victory.*

National Maritime Museum

Indeed, reading the pages of *Light Squadrons and Single Ships* in the volumes of the *Naval History of Great Britain* by William James covering the Napoleonic Wars, one is struck by the audacity of the British naval commanders to "engage the enemy more closely".

A famous quotation of Lord Nelson before the battle of Trafalgar reminded his Captains that nothing should be left to chance and that "in case Signals can neither be seen nor perfectly understood, no Captain can do very wrong if he places his Ship alongside that of an Enemy". (See Lambert A. *Nelson-Britannia's God of War.* p.291).

A Voyage Round The World in the years 1740-44 by Commodore Lord George Anson (1697-1762) gives an authentic description of the horrendous conditions at sea and the privations suffered by his men during Anson's circumnavigation. The original was compiled from the records of the voyage made by Anson, which were written up by the Rev. Richard Walter MA, Chaplain of HMS *Centurion* in that expedition and published in London in 1748.

For those unwilling to plough through all 380 pages of the book, which was re-published by Heron Books, London, in 1911, the illustrated lecture by Surgeon Vice-Admiral Sir James Watt KBE, retired Medical Director General of the Navy (1972-77), is strongly recommended. It is entitled *The medical bequest of disaster at sea: Commodore Anson's circumnavigation 1740-44* and was published in the Journal of the Royal College of Physicians of London, Vol.32 No.6 1998: pp 572-79. This account provides further proof that, even before Nelson's time, the Navy had an innate determination to succeed in spite of the deprivations of malnutrition and the multiple vitamin deficiencies of a long voyage.

CHAPTER 5:
THE IRISH CONNECTION

Although John Forbes was true Scottish by birth and nurture - probably his forbears came from the Corse and Craigievar branch of the clan - there was also an Irish branch whose family seat was at Castle Forbes in County Longford. An ancestor had been created the first Earl of Granard in 1684. Burke's Peerage and Baronetage (1876) gives details: "this is a branch of the noble Scotch [sic] family of FORBES, and its history has been fully and clearly narrated in *Memoirs of the Earls of Granard,* edited by the present Earl". [32] This is an important source, which was updated in 1868 (see later).

Sir Alexander De Forbes, Chief of the ancient Scottish House of Forbes was created a Peer of Scotland by King James II. Alexander died in 1448 and was succeeded by James, 2nd Lord Forbes. His third son, the Hon. Patrick Forbes, was armour bearer to King James III. He founded the House of Forbes of Corss [sic]. His son, David Forbes of Corss, called "Traill the Axe", was father of Patrick Forbes of Corss. His son, William Forbes of Corss had seven sons; the eldest Patrick (1564-1635), became Bishop of Aberdeen, while the sixth, Arthur, was knighted and was ancestor of the Earls of Granard in Ireland. Sir Arthur Forbes was born about the year 1569. He was Lieutenant Colonel in Forbes' regiment, which was sent to Ireland from Scotland "to quell some disturbances". In 1619, Sir Arthur was rewarded by King James I (1566-1625) of England - the 'Plantation of the County of Longford' - with 1,268 acres of land in the parish of Clongish. The Manor of Castle Forbes was built in 1624 "with the usual privileges, a Thursday's market, and a fair on St. Barthomew's Day", about 1622. *(Memoirs of the Earls of Granard,* p 31)

Sir Arthur was created a *Baronet of Nova Scotia* (see later) in 1628 but was killed in a duel at Hamburg in 1632 while his regiment was serving in Germany under the Swedish King Gustavus-Adolphus (1594-1632). Forbes' son, Sir Arthur, was born in 1623 and supported the royal cause in Scotland during the Civil War (1642-1651). In 1641, Castle Forbes, in Longford, was besieged by Irish insurgents at a time of general civil unrest. Rather in the same way as the Countess of Derby was left behind by her husband to defend Lathom House in Lancashire, while Lord Derby attended to the King's cause in the Isle of Man in 1643-45, so did Sir Arthur's heroic widow, Lady Jane Forbes with Scots troops, defend Castle Forbes "with a manly courage during nine months"(p 33). She was forced to surrender the Castle at the end of 1641 but was allowed to return to her home in Scotland.

Sir Arthur (1623-95) was rewarded after the Restoration by his appointment to the privy council of Ireland (1670) and elevated to the peerage as *Baron Clanehugh andViscount Granard* in 1673. He was marshal of the army in Ireland and, in 1684, raised the 18th Royal Irish regiment of foot, of which he was colonel-in-chief. On the 30th December of that year he was created the first Earl of Granard. Amongst his philanthropic works, he suggested to King Charles II (1630-1685) the founding of Kilmainham Hospital in Dublin for the care of Irish soldiers invalided from the Army.

"Restoration Ireland" saw a dramatic immigration of Scottish settler-landlords into Ulster and although the county of Longford is not, strictly speaking, within that province, it is in close proximity to it. Protestant settlers had been encouraged by an Act of Parliament, so that after 1662, there was an influx of English and Scottish families. Castle Forbes would have been of sturdy construction to protect its inmates from the native Irish, who resented the newcomers' advent to what they considered to be their land. King Charles II died in February 1685: these would have been precarious times for the Forbes family during the five years of Jacobite unrest, which only ended with the battle of the Boyne on 1st July 1690. In fact, Arthur the second earl (1656-1734) supported James II; having succeeded to the command of his father's regiment, was later dismissed from it by King William III (1650-1702) and was imprisoned in the Tower of London! [33]

George Forbes (1685-1765), 3rd Earl of Granard, became *Lord Forbes* in the lifetime of his father. His lordship was an eminent naval officer, who became Governor of the Leeward Islands (1729-1730) and at the time of his death was senior admiral in the Royal Navy. In 1733 he was appointed as envoy for a year to the Imperial Russian court, where he found favour with the Czarina. See *'The Command of the Ocean'* by NAM Rodger, (2004), Vol.2 1649-1815, 13, p.204.

His second son, John Forbes (1714-1796) followed his father into the British navy, where he distinguished himself in action against the combined fleets of France and Spain off Toulon in 1744 as captain of the *Norfolk*. He achieved flag rank in 1747 and was commander-in-chief in the Mediterranean two years later. He fell out with his colleagues on the Board of Admiralty by refusing to sign the death warrant for the execution of Admiral George Byng (1704-1757) at Portsmouth in 1757. On leaving the Navy in 1763, he was given command of the

Marines. In 1781, in spite of, or because of, his failure to "encourager les autres" in the court-martial of the unfortunate Byng, he was promoted to Admiral of the Fleet, which high rank he held until his death in 1765. His portrait by George Romney (1734-1802) shows the family crest and motto Fax mentis incendium gloriae. Romney was said to have painted "the face of a man not yet old, but worn and pinched". [34] [Fig 10]

Admiral Forbes, in retirement, wrote a *Memoir of the Earls of Granard* in 1770 but this lay dormant for nearly a century before it was edited and published by the seventh earl in 1868. [34]

According to this, the origin of the name *FORBES* dates from a Charter in the year 1272: Alexander the Third, King of Scotland, disposed to Fergus, son of John Forbes, the *Terras et Tenementa de Forbes* i.e. the lands and rents, to the Forbes' family of Logie adjoining the River Don in Aberdeenshire. Earlier, in the twelfth century, tradition has it that the Forbes' clan are descended from Connor Dough (the 'black Connor' in Gaelic), or O'Chonacre, whose son had arrived in Scotland from Ireland with a body of men to offer their services to the King of Scotland and, as a reward, he gave them the lands of Logie.

The first recorded Forbes was Alexander who, in 1303, stoutly defended the Castle of Urquhart, near Elgin, against Edward the First of England. When the castle was successfully stormed, Alexander and the whole garrison were killed - as was customary at that time. The Forbes family would have become extinct but, happily, his wife was pregnant and was later delivered of a son whom she named Alexander after his dead father. This Alexander loyally supported King David Bruce, until Alexander and the whole clan were slain at the Battle of Duplin [sic] in 1332.

Once again Fortune smiled on the Forbes family, as a posthumous son was born to Alexander's widow, thus ensuring the survival of the name! Named John, he was later knighted by King Robert the Second and became known as Sir John Forbes

Figure 10) The Honourable John Forbes (1714-1796)
Admiral of the Fleet.

'with the black lip' as a distinguishing sobriquet. In 1394, he was made Justiciary and Coroner for Aberdeenshire. He married Elizabeth Kennedy of Demure, of the Cassilis family, and they had four sons; the eldest, Alexander, was created 1st Lord Forbes circa 1445. [35]

George Arthur Hastings Forbes, Knight of St. Patrick, the seventh Earl of Granard in the Peerage of Ireland was Lord Lieutenant of County Leitrim and Lieutenant Colonel of the Westmeath Militia Rifles; he edited *Memoirs of the Earls of Granard*, which had originally been compiled by his ancestor Admiral George Forbes, the 3rd Earl. The revised edition was published in Dublin in 1868. The 7th Earl was obviously a scholar: he not only produced a detailed family tree (p 293) for the book but also took the trouble to establish the origin of the Forbes' name by researching the Irish genealogical archives. In particular, he mentions the controversy aroused about the identity of the 'Black Conor'. Some eminent Irish genealogists have claimed, he writes, that "the Clan Forbes was derived from the sept of MacFirbis; and it is singular that the present representatives of that sept, who live on the borders of Mayo and Sligo, all use Forbes as their name. However, Roger O'Ferrall, in his *Linea Antiqua,* deduces the origin of the Family from the Corcumroe sept of the O'Connors from the evidence of the Charter granted to Sir Fergus, grandson of the aforesaid Connor, or O'Chonacre, that the name of Forbes was a designation adopted from the lands assigned to him". Quoting from an extract of O'Ferrall's Linea Antiqua "from this Corc are O'Conor of Corcumro [in Munster]...descended, and also the ancient families of Forbess [sic] and Urquharts, in Scotland; and many other families and sirnames [sic] in Ireland and Scottland [sic] derive their pedigree from the said Corc [whose brother] Connor went into Scottland [sic] and there settled: ancestor to the noble families of Forbess [sic] and Urquhart, &c., there". This is an intriguing suggestion:

that there appears to be a strong link between the Scottish and Irish branches of the Forbes family.

Whether or not our John Forbes is descended from Sir John Forbes 'with the black lip', who flourished about the end of the 14th century in Aberdeenshire, is speculative. As far as I can ascertain from *Burke's Peerage,* there are at least two branches of the Scottish Forbes Clan, *Corse* and *Newe.* As mentioned before (p 2) John Forbes (1787-1861) was knighted for his services as Physician to Queen Victoria's Household in 1853. His coat of arms, as depicted on a family tapestry [Fig.11] with the motto *Labore Robore Spe,* gives no clue; but I am reliably informed that he was more likely sprung from the Corse branch of the family than the Newe. (Personal communication Major Sir Hamish Forbes, Bart. of Newe, Aberdeenshire).

Amongst the family papers, there is a letter, quoted in full in the *Appendix* of the *Memoirs,* p 292, by George, the 7th Earl: it is written in French - the language of the Russian Court at that time - from Anna, the Duchess of Courland to Admiral Lord Forbes. Dated 'Danzig, ce 14me Janr, 1734', it conveys the appreciation of the Czarina, as mentioned previously, for his diplomatic success at the Imperial Court. Although couched in official diplomatic phraseology, the final sentence hints that His Majesty's Plenipotentiary to the Court of Muscovy lived up to the high standards of the British Navy in personal liaisons and had made a lasting impression on at least one of the ladies of the Imperial household! Anna concludes her letter (transcribed here in contemporary French spelling and grammar):

> *"Je y joint un autre adresse dont vous vous
> pourois servie dans la suite en cas que votre
> Excellence trouve apropo de m'informe de
> quelque chosse, du reste je vous prie, my*

Lord, d'etre persuade que je suis avec au ans
de reconnoisance que de considerasion.

My Lord,
De votre Excellence,
Tres affectione amie et Servande,
La D.de Courland. "

It is worth mentioning that the Russian Court was, at that
time, experiencing one of its political upheavals in the efforts to
find an acceptable successor to Peter the Great, who had died
in 1725. Peter's niece, Anna of Courland, ruled Russia with her
unpopular German consort until Peter's daughter came to the
throne as Empress Elizabeth (1709-1762) in 1741.

Figure 11) Tapestry fire-screen showing Sir John's coat of arms
and motto Labore Robore Spe (By Work, Strength, Hope).

Forbes Family

CHAPTER 6:
FORBES: THE ROYAL NAVY 1807-1809.

We must now return to the adventures of the young John Forbes at the time of the Napoleonic Wars.

The Navy that John Forbes entered in 1807 was very different from that of his distinguished forbear, with whom he shared a name but not rank. As a result of long overdue reforms to the conditions of service in 1805, pay had been improved and the post of 'surgeon's mate' renamed 'assistant surgeon'. [36] Full surgeons now received 11 shillings per day and were entitled to half-pay on retirement. Forbes' first two years were spent in the rank of temporary assistant surgeon; this was really an apprenticeship in the trade of naval surgeon. Only the few, like Trotter and Gillespie who were genuine physicians, were treated with any professional respect but they were still called 'Surgeon'. There were 720 surgeons in the fleet in 1806, [37] so clearly young John was very low in the 'pecking order'. On obtaining the rank of 'Surgeon', he could only expect quick promotion as a result of his own exceptional ability or, possibly, temporary acting rank on the death of his superior officer in action.

While at sea, a Surgeon was expected "to keep a journal of his treatments and send it to his superiors, to send sick men to the hospital ship, or shore hospital, to supervise the general health of the ship's company, as well as those who were actually sick, and to act as adviser to the captain on matters affecting health". [38]

The discipline of keeping a journal by naval medical officers was to stand Forbes in good stead during his later years as a medical journalist in London. His main rival at that time, between 1841 and 1845, was Dr James Johnson (1777-1845). [Fig.12]. Their naval and subsequent careers had much in common. Johnson was born on a small farm in Northern Ireland; after a sound education there, he emigrated and worked as an apothecary's assistant in London before passing the examinations of the Surgeon's Hall and enlisting in the Royal Navy as a surgeon's mate in 1798. Promoted to full surgeon in 1800, he served in HMS *Caroline* in the Far East. [39] See '*The War for all the Oceans*' by Roy and Lesley Adkins, (2006), 16, p.354.

John Forbes' first two years in the Royal Navy were spent on board the *Royal George*. She was a 100-gun Ship-of-the-Line or Line-of-Battle-Ship with three decks, whose 2286 tons had cost £24.10.0. per ton. [40] Launched at Chatham dockyard to replace her predecessor of the same name, which had foundered at Spithead in 1782, she was one of the last of the 100-gun ships built in 1788 to the design of Thomas Slade of Deptford. Her sails weighed nearly 10 tons and covered an area of more than two acres. [41] Forbes joined the *Royal George* on 11 June 1807, when his ship was part of the Channel Fleet, whose main purpose was to blockade the enemy ports, especially Brest in northwest France. In addition to conventional 16 and 32 pounder 'long guns', she was armed with 16 carronades: these were short guns of large bore, named after a town in Central Scotland, where they were produced at a large ironworks. They were introduced gradually to the Fleet as, initially, many tended to burst apart on firing. [42] Credit for their general adoption must

Figure 12) James Johnson (1777-1845).
Lithograph by T Brigford.

Wellcome Library, London

be given to Sir Charles Middleton (1726-1813), [Fig.13] Controller of the Navy, 1778-90. [43] Later, as First Lord of the Admiralty from April 1805, he was instrumental in issuing orders, which set the stage for the Battle of Trafalgar in October. [44] But, firstly, in combination with Nelson, he had ensured the safety of the Mediterranean and prevented a French invasion. He became Lord Barham in May 1805.

While constantly cruising between the Scilly Islands and Ushant, the fleet guarded against any attempt by Napoleon to embark his invasion barges from Boulogne and the other channel ports. *The Grande Armée* may have been effective in winning French victories on the dry land of the Continent but British sea power held it at bay at this critical period. In the words of the great American admiral and naval historian Alfred Mahan (1840-1914), writing in 1890 on the influence of Sea Power upon History: "those far distant, storm-beaten ships upon which the Grand Army never looked, stood between it and the dominion of the world". [45]

The blockade of the French ports not only prevented the emergence of their battle fleets but also stifled their civilian trade and prevented the export of French industrial products. (It also led indirectly to a sense of isolation on the part of England from the rest of continental Europe, which has persisted to the present day). To the twenty-year-old John Forbes, such weighty matters were of no concern compared to the daily routine of life at sea and learning the skills of a naval surgeon. He might just have been aware that the main purpose of the Channel Fleet, apart from its essential role in 'Defence' and 'Command of the Seas', was in protecting trade: East India ships and other merchantmen were vulnerable to large enemy vessels so that, since the mid-eighteenth century, it had been the policy to maintain a 'Western Squadron' at sea for 'Trade-protection'. [46]

Figure 13) Admiral Charles Middleton (1726-1813).

National Maritime Museum

As regards 'Defence' there was still in 1807 the ever-present threat of invasion from a French conquest of Ireland. [By 1807, the Emperor Napoleon, victorious in continental Europe, was again considering invasion of the British Isles.] To quote James: "Napoleon, it will be recollected, in his plan of operations against England, framed in September, 1804, intended that the Brest fleet, of 23 sail of the line and smaller vessels, should disembark 30,000 to 40,000 men in the north of Ireland, or even in Scotland, in order to operate as a diversion while the main body of the grand army was traversing the Channel. Some distinguished French officers, it seems, were of the opinion, "that Ireland solely should have been the object of the expedition, judging that, with the aid of the disaffected inhabitants of that unhappy country, a third of the army assembled for the conquest of England would suffice; that the troops in their diminished number could be transported by a fleet of men-of-war, instead of having to wait for so many contingencies to concur, ere a flotilla of 2000 gun-boats could reach in safety the opposite coast; and that the loss of Ireland would inflict a deep wound in the pride of England, would weaken her resources, and greatly reduce her in the scale of national importance". [47] This invasion via the back door was, and remained even as recently as 1940, a constant worry to Whitehall and to the Admiralty in particular.

Besides, the Navy in early 1807, had other commitments: Lord Collingwood's squadron still kept watch off Cadiz and, in addition, there were the ports of Brest and Toulon to be blockaded. When the French tried to persuade Turkey to enter the war on the side of Napoleon in 1807, HMS *Royal George,* flying the flag of Vice-Admiral Sir John Duckworth (1748-1817), was detached from Collingwood to the Aegean; there she joined a British squadron of six ships of the line in a bold attempt to force a passage through the Dardanelles in order to threaten the Turkish capital. During February/March of that year, in spite of reaching the Sea of Marmora, getting within eight miles of Constantinople, and engaging the small Turkish fleet, this expedition failed in its political objective of prising the Turks from their French alliance. Although no Royal Navy line-of-battle ships were sunk, the structural damage inflicted by the Turkish shore batteries on running the gauntlet through the narrows, added to the losses of British officers, marines and seamen on board were disproportionately high compared to the destruction of a 64-gun Turkish man-of-war and "three or four frigates". [48]

The *Royal George* was next involved in an expedition to capture Alexandria in Egypt. Duckworth's squadron escorted 33 troop transports from Messina but within 24 hours they were scattered by bad weather. Eventually, on the 22nd March, he reached Aboukir Bay; troops were landed but, although Alexandria surrendered, the later campaign was not a success. Duckworth departed for England, where he arrived on 26th May 1807. [49]

Sir John was criticized on his return home for not having concluded a treaty with the Ottoman Porte and for only getting within eight miles of the capital; but conditions of wind and tide were not in his favour in the Sea of Marmora. There was no doubting his courage for he had received a gold medal in 1794. His squadron had been badly mauled during the hazardous passage through the Dardanelles, where he had been unaware that the forts had been strengthened by the French. But he had lost no ships, had silenced the batteries of the castles of Sestos and Abydos and destroyed a squadron of Turkish frigates. No harm came to his career as a result of these two expeditions as he was promoted to full Admiral in 1810 and created a baronet in 1813. [50] However, his conduct at the Sea of Marmora has been ridiculed. [51]

Such was the background to John Forbes joining Royal George on 11th June 1807 at Plymouth as part of the Channel

Fleet. She had a crew of 850 men and was armed with 104 guns and was classed as a First Rate.

At the time that Forbes joined Royal George, she was lying alongside the 'Hulk' *Yarmouth* in the stretch of water known as the *Hamoaze* at the mouth of the river Tamar off Plymouth dockyard. [52]

With the help of artificers, shipwrights and joiners from the dockyard, *Royal George's* ship's company carried out refitting work on the ship's hull and rigging; she had suffered extensive damage from Turkish gunfire during her passage under the forts of the Dardanelles as part of Sir Thomas Duckworth's squadron and on her return had put in to Spithead before sailing down the coast to Cawsand Bay. [This anchorage was used before the building of the breakwater across Plymouth Sound.] While repairs took place, the ship's company lived on board the hulk.

At the beginning of July general stores, guns and ammunition were embarked in preparation for putting to sea again to join the Channel Fleet via Torbay. On 13th November 1807, flying the flag of Vice-Admiral Duckworth, she sailed "to join the fleet" off Ushant. The next six weeks were spent patrolling the Western Approaches between the Isle of Ushant and The Lizard during which time "strange sails" were sighted and examined as part of the blockade process. She experienced strong winds during which her mainsails were carried away but her rigging was repaired at sea. She returned to Torbay at the end of December 1807.

This 'sea-time' would have been a useful introduction for Assistant Surgeon (Temporary) John Forbes to the ways of the Navy and the general chaos below decks during a storm at sea. He would have found his 'sea-legs' and found his personal remedy for seasickness!

In mid-January 1808, *Royal George* formed part of a squadron which sailed westwards for the West Indies; the weather was kind and, picking up the trade winds, she logged between 140 and 170 miles a day to reach St. Kitts on 17 February. She cruised around the various islands for the next few weeks but did not encounter any enemy ships before returning to Cawsand Bay, near Plymouth in mid-April. By mid-June she was patrolling off Ushant again for a month or so before returning to Torbay; this was the pattern for the rest of the year, except for one occasion in September, when she received a signal that "the enemy are out" and spent some time stationed off Brest but without sighting any French ships.

During these relatively uneventful periods, John Forbes must have carried out his duties well, for on 3rd February 1809 -with seniority 27th January 1809 - he was promoted to Full Surgeon. He was discharged from the ship after serving for nearly 21 months; the rest of the crew were 'paid off' on 31st March 1809. [53]

At least he probably would not have had to deal with cases of the dreaded scurvy. Following Lind's work, the significance of which was belatedly appreciated by the Admiralty, lemon juice had been introduced to the Fleet in 1795. Prior to that, 'Malt Wort' had been used at the suggestion of Dr David MacBride (born in County Antrim in 1726). He had influential friends at the Admiralty but, as has been pointed by Sir James Watt, the policy of having malt wort, i.e. fermented maltose, adopted as the main antiscorbutic at sea "condemned thousands of sailors to death until Sir Gilbert Blane, a disciple of Lind, used his influence to make lemon juice generally available to the Fleet". (Ref: 24, p 578). This simple measure caused the elimination of scurvy within a year!

By 1800 the Navy was capable of maintaining fleets at sea for long periods off Brest and Cadiz. Sir Gilbert Blane (1749-1834) had sailed with Admiral Rodney to the West Indies in 1779, where he saw the high mortality in the Fleet from sickness, including scurvy. He published his *Observations on the Diseases of Seamen* in 1783. Later, when he became head of the Naval Medical Board, he introduced the compulsory use of lemon juice. The triumvirate of Blane, Trotter and Gillespie, formed a vitally important influence on the favourable development of naval medicine at the commencement of the Napoleonic Wars. However, scurvy was still a problem in the blockading ships of the Channel Fleet as recently as October 1806, when four ships of a squadron off Brest had to put in to Falmouth with suspected cases of the disease. 'This was later attributed to 'malignant ulcers' by Surgeon William Beatty (1733-1842), at that time Physician to the Channel Fleet, in a dispute with the ship's surgeon of HMS *Gibraltar*. See 'Nelson's Surgeon' by Brockliss, Cardwell and Moss,(2008) 5, p.163.

CHAPTER 7:
ACTION IN THE CARIBBEAN

John Forbes' name next appears on the books of HMS *Royal William* on 12th February 1809. 54 She had been launched at Portsmouth in 1719 and classed as a First Rate 100 guns (three-decker) but was never fitted to go to sea; in 1756 she was re-classified as a Second Rate of 84 guns. Taken out of service finally in 1790, she was used as a 'Receiving Ship' at Portsmouth. 55 A Receiving Ship was used for the temporary accommodation for officers and men before they were drafted to ships. 56

Forbes joined HMS *Castor* from *Royal William* on 23 February 1809 "for passage to the Leeward Islands". 57 A small but fast 'Fifth Rate', she had been launched at Harwich in May 1785 and had a crew of 220 men. 58 Normally, she would have had on board a Surgeon and his Assistant but, on this occasion, she carried some Supernumerary Surgeons, besides three Lieutenants and forty Marines, as reinforcements for Admiral Cochrane's squadron on the Leeward Islands Station. 59

The conditions on board *Castor* were very different from those in a line-of-battle ship like *Royal George*. As there were other Surgeons aboard, John Forbes may have spent time 'brushing up' on the experience of other naval medical officers in the Caribbean. We know that amongst the large collection of books that he donated to Marischal College at Aberdeen in 1859, there were two works by Dr Leonard Gillespie (1758-1842).[60] Gillespie had attended hospitals in London, Edinburgh and Paris and served as Nelson's Physician of the Fleet during the months just prior to the Battle of Trafalgar but resigned due to ill health. He was highly regarded by the Admiral. Previously (1796-1802) he had been Surgeon-in-Charge of the Naval Hospital at Martinique. There Gillespie dealt with an epidemic of Yellow Fever on the West Indies station – a disease with a high mortality.[61]

James Lind had written his classic *Treatise of the Scurvy* in 1753 and followed with *An Essay on the Most Effectual Means of Preserving the Health of Seamen in the Royal Navy* in 1757, while acting as Physician at the Royal Naval Hospital, Haslar. These works would have formed essential vade mecums for any ambitious young naval surgeon anxious to progress by "bloody wars" for "quick promotion". Again, we know that Forbes' library of his mature years contained both volumes. Whether or not their pages were well-thumbed and stained by salt spray is a matter for conjecture but doubtless, by this time (1809), Lind's suggestions on naval hygiene and the supply of lemon juice in water or spirits would have been mandatory on any long voyage. [62]

Castor sailed in early March 1809 from Spithead with a convoy of merchant ships and arrived at Carlisle Bay, off Bridgetown, Barbados on 11/12th April. On the 13th, she sailed as escort to a convoy to Dominica in the Leewards. [Fig.14].

Simultaneously, possibly unknown to those on board *Castor*, a British force of 2,000 to 3,000 men, escorted by a small naval squadron under the command of Captain Philip Beavor of the 40-gun frigate *Acasta*, were landed on the two small islands of Les Saintes at the southern tip of the French island of Guadeloupe. This area is famous in the historiography of the Royal Navy as being the scene of Admiral George Rodney's (1719-

*Figure 14) Map of Caribbean including the Leeward
Islands and Puerto Rico, with insert of Antigua,
Guadeloupe & Dominica.*

1792) decisive victory over the French Admiral de Grasse in April 1782, which prevented a French attack on Jamaica. [63]

To return to the amphibious combined operation on the 14th April 1809: during the afternoon the soldiers, marines and seamen were able "with some difficulty" [a laconic understatement] to drag two 8-inch guns up an 800 feet high mountain overlooking three French line-of-battle ships in the harbour below. The ensuing bombardment resulted in forcing these vessels to put to sea at 8 pm that evening, where they remained under the guns of Rear Admiral Sir Alexander Cochrane's (1758-1832) squadron. He flew his flag in the 98-gun *Neptune*; the squadron also included the 74-gun *Pompée* (Captain WC Fahie) and the 18-gun brig-sloop *Recruit* (Captain Charles Napier). During the "unusually dark" night of the 14/15th April, the three enemy ships made for the open sea and, in the confusion of a night action, succeeded in making their escape pursued by the *Recruit* and the *Pompée*. [64] [*Pompée* was an ex-French '74' captured at the blockade of Toulon in 1793, when her captain defected to the British].

CHAPTER 8:
THE FINAL ACTION OFF PUERTO RICO

Meanwhile, Forbes and his shipmates in *Castor* were sailing some six miles out to sea when, in the early evening of the 14th, they heard gunfire and the lookout reported several rockets to starboard. She immediately 'cleared for action' but it was not until daylight on the following morning that the enemy ships were sighted sailing on a northwesterly course. Following a signal from the flagship, *Castor* joined in the chase; later two of the French ships altered course to the west-southwest and escaped. (They eventually arrived home safely at Cherbourg). A third vessel was not so lucky: this was the 74-gun *D'Hautpoult*. She sailed on a northwesterly course hotly pursued by *Pompée* and *Recruit*. In the meantime, during the forenoon of 15th April, *Castor* joined the flagship *Neptune* and the rest of the squadron in the chase. At 4 am on the same day the *Recruit* " by her superior sailing again got near enough to discharge a broadside at the *D'Haupolt* [sic], now the rearmost French ship; and the *Pompée* was very soon in a situation to open a distant fire from her bow-chasers". Napier in the *Recruit* bravely continued to engage the *D'Hautpolt* throughout daylight on the 15th and she, inevitably, lost some of her rigging and sails from French gunfire and so was forced to fall astern; it was at 8 pm that the French ships finally separated. During the afternoon of the 15th, *Pompée* "fired several guns at the enemy" but *Castor* and the other ships in the pursuing squadron did not engage. [65]

The chase continued throughout the night; at times *Castor* lost sight of the other ships in Cochrane's squadron but she remained in contact with the enemy. By dawn on the 16th, with the high land of Puerto Rico in sight, she was sailing in fresh breezes about five miles astern of *D'Hautpoult* and Captain William Roberts ordered all sail to be set. By midnight she "had got so far ahead as to be on the starboard bow of the *Pompée* that, at 2.45 am on the 17th, she shortened sail and brought the enemy to bear within little more than half a mile to port. Captain Roberts ordered, "beat to quarters" and opened fire with the "larboard guns". [12 pounders]. Being a Fifth Rate, Forbes' action station in the lowest orlop deck would have been a makeshift operating 'cockpit' with no after cabins. [66] Two sea chests would have been brought together to make a crude operating table and instruments and ligatures laid out for amputations; the surgeons would probably have available a copy of William Northcote's textbook of surgery (1770). It is not hard to imagine what was going through young Forbes' mind as he crouched with his colleagues in the semi-darkness of the cramped rolling mess-deck listening to the loud crash of the guns, the shaking of the deckheads and the general tumult of a warship in action but, all the time, ignorant of the events transpiring on the upper decks.

According to James, what was happening after 3 am on the 17th April was: "the action was maintained between an English 12-pounder frigate and a French 74 until 4 am". By then the *Pompée* had overtaken *Castor* "when the action became general". James' account continues: "the *Pompée* engaged the *D'Hautpoult* within musket-shot distance, gradually closing until 5h.15m. am, when the *D'Hautpoult* ranged ahead, steering before the wind, and became again engaged with the *Castor*. Before many shots had been engaged between these unequal antagonists, the *Pompée*, putting her helm a-port, fired her bow guns at, and was preparing, with her broadside to rake, the *D'Hautpoult*, when the French ship, now a complete wreck in rigging and sails, lowered her topsails, hove to, and hauled down her colours." [67]

Clowes, in his account of the action in *The Royal Navy Vol. V* London 1900; Sampson Low, Marston & Co. pp 435-36, gives credit to Captain Roberts and *Castor* for delaying the French 74 so much by her gunfire that *Pompée* was able to catch up and bring the enemy to close action. He recorded that the French casualties amounted to between 80 and 90 in killed and wounded out of a crew of 680 men and boys (p 436). HMS *Castor* had suffered very little structural damage in the two-hour night action and had lost only one seaman killed and six wounded, so Forbes and his surgical colleagues escaped lightly. (The total British casualties in the squadron amounted to 10 killed and 35 wounded.)

Castor and *Pompée* were soon joined by the rest of the squadron, including the flagship *Neptune* and the *Recruit* whose sails, riddled by French fire, bore witness to her harrying pursuit in the early part of the action. For his bravery, Rear-Admiral Cochrane promoted Napier to command the French prize *D'Hautpoult* "on the spot". She was a fine ship of 1871 tons and was taken by her prize crew to the nearest English harbour at Antigua for repairs. She later served in the British fleet as HMS Abercrombie. [68]

According to the Captain's log of *Castor*, the *D'Hautpoult* surrendered after a broadside from the English frigate: there is no doubt that she was closely engaged up until the French struck her colours. [69] The log goes on to say that, after midday, 23 French prisoners were taken on board, while 5 supernumerary midshipmen and one lieutenant were discharged to the *Neptune*.

Forbes would have emerged from the gloom of the lower deck to find victory completed and to learn that, on a direct order from the flagship, he was to be transferred to the D'Hautpolt to help the French surgeons with their wounded. [70] (This was probably because Forbes was the only surgeon available who could speak French so that he was the obvious choice to help the defeated enemy). Having lost supernumerary surgeon Forbes, *Castor* made some repairs at sea and returned to Barbados with the French prisoners of war.

Surgeon Forbes remained on board the French prize, when she was taken to Antigua and there she was repaired and purchased for the Royal Navy. He remained on her books from 17 April to 10 May 1809, when he joined the 12-gun brig, *Netley* at Antigua. [71]

CHAPTER 9:
A WEST INDIAN IDYLL

John Forbes joined HMS *Netley* in Freeman's Bay, Antigua, during the morning of 10 May 1809. [72] Originally an American brig, she had been launched in 1804 and named after the hunter Nimrod. She had been purchased in 1808 as a fast sailing ship to carry urgent messages or men and was commanded by a Lieutenant. [73] She was armed with ten 12 pounder and two 6 pounder guns and had a crew of 65 men. [74] She was the smallest vessel in which Forbes had, so far, served.

While at Antigua, *Netley* embarked sufficient provisions for a three months' voyage, made some repairs and, generally, made ready to go to sea. She sailed on the 14th May for St.Croix in the Virgin Islands but stopped for a few hours at Sandy Point, St.Kitts en route. During the passage *Netley* pursued any "strange sail" and, if not British, it would be boarded in order to examine the Captain's papers and ship's cargo. These routine checks would sometimes annoy "neutrals", especially the Americans, particularly if any of the crew were "pressed" into the Royal Navy. Forbes would have examined any such new recruits and reported to the captain of *Netley* any seaman he deemed unfit.

St.Croix was reached on 22 May. The brig next had a refit: her guns, shot and provisions were landed ashore, rigging was stripped and the hold cleared and cleaned. On the following day, alongside the wharf, all hands worked at "getting the ballast out". The ship's hull was painted and her "copper-bottoming" renewed. All this work was done by the ship's company working in the heat of the day. One can well imagine the cursing as men were 'started' by the petty officers. Unsurprisingly, it took the best part of four weeks before she was ready to put to sea again.

Although he probably played no direct part in all this activity, Surgeon Forbes - by now gaining in medical/surgical confidence every day - may well have been interested in how much a small ship like the *Netley* could be refitted independently of the nearest dockyard at Barbados or English Harbour at Antigua. For painting and coppering, the brig would have been heeled over, first one way and then the other by sheer manpower. Anyone who has ever maintained even a small yacht will appreciate the work involved! Brian Lavery has pointed out that since the American War of Independence (1775-83), the Navy had adopted the policy of copper sheathing all ships' bottoms. [75] This stopped the growth of seaweed and increased the speed of the ship; it also protected against the eating through the timbers by the notorious shipworm. "Coppering" had the dual advantages of protection and of making it possible for ships to remain at sea for longer spells away from major dockyards.

On the 18th June *Netley* resumed the pleasant task of patrolling among the Virgin Islands. She anchored off St.Thomas for a week and, no doubt, Forbes was able to indulge his passion for swimming; the warm clear waters would have contrasted with the frigid North Sea waters of Sandend Bay near his home in Banffshire. He had been a strong swimmer since his schooldays and is said to have saved the life of a shipmate "in the West Indies". [76] [The Captain's Log of *Netley* does not record this but it may have taken place elsewhere in the Caribbean].

For the rest of July, she cruised off the islands including Saba to the northwest of St.Kitts. She returned to St.Croix in the first week of August. John Forbes kept to this leisurely way of life for the rest of his commission on board *Netley*. The brig cruised around the islands of the northern Caribbean for three or four weeks at a time then anchored at such places as St.Croix, St.Thomas, Tortola and English Harbour, Antigua, before going back to patrolling at sea. Although some ships were boarded, no enemy vessels were encountered. After surviving the 'Hurricane Season' from August to October without mishap, Forbes left the ship at Antigua on 6 March 1810 but was present on board at the capture of Guadeloupe by the British on 5 February 1810, thus entitling him to a clasp to his Naval General Service medal.

On the following day the Scottish surgeon arrived on board HMS *Cherub* at anchor in Freeman's Bay, Antigua. [77] She was a 16 gun Ship Sloop with a crew of 125: slightly larger than *Netley*, she had been built at Dover and launched in 1806.[78] [During the period after the declaration of war against Napoleon in May 1803, the Leeward Islands squadron had been built up so that, by 1805, there were six ships of the line, thirteen frigates and the same number of sloops] [79]

Once again Forbes had the opportunity to relax in a small ship at the expense of His Majesty King George III. According to Parkes, Forbes was, at this time: "...about the middle height, and was strongly and squarely built; he had blue eyes, a bright florid complexion, and was full of spirits, frank and joyous. His manner was bluff and hearty, but pleasing, from the evidence it gave of sincerity and goodness. His habits were extremely active". [80] Far from being a dour introverted Scotsman, this describes a very fit boisterous character, keen to play his part in all the activities of a ship at sea, perhaps even prepared to take part in watch-keeping duties with the other officers?

Parkes goes on to say that Forbes used his spare time in the Navy to augment his knowledge of the French, German and Italian languages as well as of the Classics. He would have been on close terms with his fellow officers, particularly any who shared his intellectual interests. This agreeable life was spoilt when "...after several months in a small sloop", he quarrelled with the "young officer in command", so that the Scot was forced "to his books for society and change". [81]

He had joined *Cherub* on 7th March, whose captain would have held the rank of 'Commander'. [The rank of 'Master and Commander' dated from the late 17th century; in 1794 the term 'Master' was dropped in favour of the simple rank of 'Commander' but the description 'Master's Log' continued. [82]] The Master's Log for *Cherub* has been difficult to read. (personal communication GK Salt). It seems that *Cherub*, after spending two days taking on stores at Antigua, sailed for the island of Guadeloupe, captured earlier by the British in 1810. She carried supplies for Cochrane's squadron at anchor off Basse Terre and delivered these on 10th March. After a week there, she returned to Antigua. The next few months were spent on routine patrolling duties with no mention of any encounters with the enemy. It may well have been during this commission that John Forbes wrote a *Report on the Meterology of the West Indies,* which is mentioned in Parkes'*Memoir* 1862. [84] But, like the poems he wrote at sea, which were said to have been published in the local West Indian press, no trace of these has been found. [85]

On the 13th July 1810 Forbes joined HMS *Vimiera* at 'The Saints' off the southern tip of Guadeloupe. [86] He replaced Surgeon Robert Hamilton, who had been sentenced on the previous day to dismissal from the Service by a court martial.

Vimiera was a 16 gun brig with a crew of 100 men. She was armed with twelve 24 pounder guns and four 6 pounders. She was originally the French corvette Le Pylade built at Le Havre in 1804 but captured by HMS *Pompée* to the east of Barbados in October 1808. [87] It seems possible that she was re-named in honour of General Arthur Wellesley's first victory over the French under Junot in the Peninsular war at the Portugese town of Vimiero on 21st August of the same year. [88]

On the 14th she sailed to Basseterre Roads, St.Kitts and anchored there after a swift passage. Surgeon John Forbes was ordered to return home to Portsmouth in *Vimiera* via Bermuda. During the next four weeks at sea, he would have observed the daily routine of a man-o'-war: decks were scrubbed, ship's boats repaired and damaged sails mended. Occasionally a live animal, such as a bullock, was killed for fresh meat and a seaman was flogged for some breach of discipline: such was naval life.

By the 20/21st July *Vimiera* had made good progress towards Bermuda, logging about 130 miles a day without incident. It is easy to picture her sailing close-hauled as nearly into the wind as possible, with the spray flying over her scrubbed decks and leaving a wake of white water astern. After a short stay to replenish stores and water, she set a course for home and arrived at Spithead on 16th August. John Forbes remained on board until discharged on 31st August 1810. [89]Meanwhile the brig moved into Portsmouth dockyard in order to land her stores and guns. On 1st September the ship's company were discharged (with no shore leave) to HMS *Hibernia*, where they were urgently needed to man this big 110-gun three-decker in the same class as the *Royal George*. 90 On the same day *Vimiera's* commissioning pendant, which distinguished a warship from a merchantman, was hauled down. (She was laid up and finally sold off in 1814).

Before disembarking for his well-earned shore leave, Forbes may have glanced over the anchorage and seen HMS *Royal William* from where he had joined *Castor* for passage to the Leewards eighteen months previously. He may not have known -

or even cared - that the 'Receiving Ship' had ended her active life in 1790 and that she was only retained on the Navy List because King George III was said to be particularly fond of her! [91]

Before ending this chapter on Forbes on the Leewards Islands station, it is worth mentioning that French and American privateers were a constant menace to merchantmen in that area. [A privateer being a privately owned war vessel with a special licence to capture enemy ships and sell their cargoes.] The hand written Master's Log (NA ADM 52/2205) of HMS *Cherub* is indistinct but it seems that she patrolled via the Mona Passage between Santo Domingo and Puerto Rico to Nassau in the Bahamas. It seems very likely that she may have been under orders to search for and report on any lurking privateers.

CHAPTER 10:
MEDICAL OFFICER AT HASLAR

No details are available as to how or where Forbes spent his leave of absence from the Navy between September and the end of December 1810. We do know that he joined the staff at the Royal Naval Hospital Haslar, Gosport, on 6th January 1811 and was discharged on 7th April. [92] "Haslar", as it was commonly referred to in the Navy, had been built, along with the other naval hospital at Plymouth, to improve the shore facilities for the 'Sick and Hurt' seamen under overall control of the Admiralty in London. Previously, they had been sent ashore to privately owned hospitals or houses but this practice often lead to drunkenness and desertion. [93]

The naval hospital at Greenwich had been used since the end of the seventeenth century but Haslar was authorised by King George II in September 1744. [94] It was opened for patients in 1754 and, by the end of the century, was staffed by one physician, one surgeon and six assistants, one visiting apothecary and four dispensers. Apart from the medical/surgical staff, there was a regular Royal Naval captain and four lieutenants to maintain discipline. There were about 1200 beds or 'cots' in naval parlance, and a capacity to treat 15,000 patients a year. [95] Dr James Lind had been appointed Physician-in-Charge in 1758 and successfully combined the duties of naval surgeon, physician and administrator; simultaneously, he found time to revise his work *An Essay on the effectual means of preserving the health of Seamen in the Royal Navy* (1762), first published in 1757. A third edition (1774) stressed the importance of hygiene in the treatment of fevers. One of Lind's chief contributions to the well being of his patients at Haslar was to lay down clear regulations on the dispensing of medicines, including antiscorbutics. [96] Three years after his death in 1794, no cases of scurvy could be found in the hospital. [97] [This was the result of Gilbert Blane's pressure on the Admiralty belatedly to implement Lind's practical recommendations made many years before. Blane was made a baronet in 1812. Four years before his death in 1834, he founded a prize in the shape of two gold medals to be awarded biennially to 'Medical Officers of the Royal Navy', who were considered to have contributed most towards the health of the Navy.]

By the time of Forbes' arrival in the winter of 1811, the hospital routine was well established. He developed an increasing interest in Medicine ('Physic') rather than Surgery, which was to lead to his graduation as MD of the University of Edinburgh some six years later. At Haslar, he would have dealt with a wide range of naval medical disorders such as pulmonary tuberculosis ('consumption' or 'phthisis') and rheumatic heart disease; Forbes would have had opportunities to discuss medical cases with colleagues - a welcome 'refresher course. Pulmonary 'consumption' was also increasing among recruits serving on the Channel Station and, by 1806-09, death rates in hospitals far exceeded those from scurvy.

He would have visited the patients under his care at least twice a day and reported to his senior medical officer any whom he considered should be discharged fully fit to go back to sea or who were downgraded 'fit for shore duties only'. In some cases of severe illness or injury, names would have to be submitted for

permanent invaliding from the Service. Food and living accommodation would have been palatial compared to the Spartan
conditions afloat and, altogether, his three months at Haslar
would have been a stimulating period, both mentally and phys-
ically. Three years later when he joined the 74-gun ship-of-the-
line HMS *Venerable* in February 1814, it was with a 'recommend
in Surgery' and a 'good recommend in Physic'. [98]

The present Admiralty Librarian has found that the Physicians at Haslar in early 1811 were Drs. R Wright and J Gray and
the Surgeons were Duncan M'Arthur, Charles Dods and Joseph
Stevenson. John Forbes, with the other resident doctors, would
have benefited from 'updating' in contemporary Medicine and
Surgery, as well as in the methods of the Navy. The senior
physician, Wright, was paid £766 10s per annum, the junior,
Gray, £600 and the three surgeons £500 each. (Personal
communication, Mrs J.V.S. Wickenden, Institute of Naval
Medicine, Gosport.)

Professor Carpenter of Cambridge has described (1986)
James Lind's work at Haslar on the prevention of scurvy in the
years before his retirement from the Navy in 1783. In a Table
from his book *The History of Scurvy and Vitamin C*, Carpenter
has analysed traditional antiscorbutics and gives the highest
value of 240mg/100ml to Lind's 'Rob' of concentrated orange
juice. [99] John Forbes and his colleagues at Haslar were fortunate
that the problem of scurvy had been solved just in time to
maintain the continental blockade, whereas the French navy
lagged behind. [100]

A recent article (2002) in the *Journal of the Royal Naval
Medical Service* gives a fascinating account of the catastrophic
effect of scurvy on the Swedish Fleet in 1808. [101] A letter from
Surgeon John Jamison to Admiral Sir James Saumarez (1757-
1836) written on board HMS *Victory* at Carlscrona, dated 16th
October 1808, recommending the use of fresh vegetables and

lemon juice (quoting ADM 1/7, 278-9) is quoted fully on pp 121-22. An alternative view has recently (2004) been expressed by NAM Rodger and others that "the significance of scurvy [in the Navy] has been grossly exaggerated". See: *The Great Wheels of Commerce and War, Administration 1715-1763*. In: *The Command of the Ocean*. A Naval History of Britain, 1649-1815. London (2004): Penguin Books Ltd., chapter **19**, p 308.

The same author mentions that the cost of building Haslar was more than £100,000; for this considerable sum the Admiralty was recompensed by the "highest standards of medical care, careful segregation of infectious diseases and (not least) careful guard against the risk of desertion (p 309). The provisions for the 'Sick and Hurt' were expanded in the naval hospital at Plymouth, which was opened for the reception of patients from nearby Stonehouse Creek in the early 1760s. Rodger remarks that the innovative design of separate blocks at Plymouth was copied on the continent of Europe.

Finally, it should be pointed out that it was not until the 1930s that the discovery of Vitamin C provided the researchers with the specific antiscorbutic to finally defeat scurvy.

CHAPTER 11:
THE NORTH SEA SQUADRON 1811-13

At the end of April 1811 John Forbes embarked upon one of the most challenging of his commissions in the Royal Navy, exchanging the sunlit blue waters of the Caribbean for the cold gray of the North Sea. He joined HMS *Desirée* on the 29th April off the Dutch coast in the region of the island of Texel. He had sailed on the day before in a cutter, HMS *Idas*, from Yarmouth Roads (Norfolk). *Desirée* was originally a 36 gun French frigate built at Dunkirk in 1796 but she had been captured in July 1800 by HM Sloop Dart in a 'cutting out' operation and retained her previous French name. [103] Her armament had been increased to 40 guns, comprising twenty-eight 24 pounder long guns and twelve 32-pounder carronades for close quarters actions. She had a crew of 264 men and formed part of the Texel and Scheldt force of 27 ships of the line, 5 frigates and 12 sloops engaged on blockading the main entrances to the Dutch ports. [104] This squadron included the '74s' *Defiance* and *Bellerophon*, both of which had fought under Nelson at Trafalgar. Captain Durham of HMS *Defiance* captured the French line-of-battle-ship *L'Aigle*, but she was wrecked in the storm after the battle. [105] It was to HMS *Bellerophon* that Napoleon Bonaparte finally surrendered at Rochefort after Waterloo (1815). Known in the Navy as 'Billy Ruff'n', she had fought at the Nile in 1798.

John Forbes, fresh from his stimulating time at Haslar Hospital, would have had to settle down to the boring routine of patrolling off the Dutch coast of Texel and Camperdown, the latter being the scene of his fellow-Scotsman's, Admiral Adam Duncan, (1731-1804), [Fig.15] decisive victory over the Dutch fleet, under Jan Willem de Winter (1750-1812), in 1797.

Forbes and his naval surgical colleagues would have enjoyed the improved status and pay, which were introduced belatedly in 1806. This followed from reports of inadequate numbers of surgeons to deal with casualties at Camperdown. [106] After this victory, the Royal Navy kept up a constant blockade of Dutch commerce by the squadron of the North Sea Fleet based at Yarmouth. In particular, they blockaded the Dutch naval bases and the exits from the ports of Amsterdam and Antwerp via the Texel channel and the mouth of the river Scheldt at Flushing. On average there were usually ten warships on patrol and another small squadron of frigates and brigs were placed at the mouths of the rivers Elbe and Weser during the Spring to Autumn. On the 18th May, there was a brief skirmish off "Yelland" (? Vlieland, near Texel) between some Dutch gunboats and *Desirée*'s launch and cutter but with no damage or casualties. At the end of May, she returned to Yarmouth Roads to repair her rigging, paint ship and take on board fresh provisions and supplies both for *Desirée* and the other ships of the squadron; after twelve days she returned on patrol.

On the 7th August: "John O'Sullivan, seaman, fell from the main topsail yard on Mr Morrison, Midshipman, and both were severely injured". The outcome is not recorded but, no doubt, Surgeon John Forbes was involved in treating the unfortunate men.

For the rest of the year, *Desirée* spent her time sailing between Yarmouth Roads and the Texel; at the end of 1811, she anchored

Figure 15) Admiral Duncan

National Maritime Museum

off Lowestoft. The ensuing year was to see France's attack on Russia, after the Czar's decision to admit neutral shipping to his ports, including American trading for the British, contrary to the 'Continental System' of blockade devised by Napoleon.

The start of the year 1812 saw a resumption of routine patrolling off the Texel channel and the mouth of the Scheldt at Flushing. "Strange Sails" were sighted and sometimes boarded but they usually proved to be innocent merchantmen going about their "lawful occasions". Excitement occurred on one occasion, when the ship sighted proved to be the USS *Constitution;* the presence of an American warship so close to the Dutch coast must have caused some surprise. The Log does not say whether or not the 'Yankee' was boarded in order to examine her papers and cargo for contraband. It was also customary at that time to search for alleged British citizens and deserters from the Royal Navy; the interference with American trade and the impressment of its seamen were causes of the War of 1812 between the two countries. It was said that the United States held records of 6257 Americans impressed into the British navy and there may well have been many unrecorded cases. [107] The USS *Constitution* along with her sister ship the *United States* had been launched in 1797 to protect American merchantmen from the French and the ravages of the corsairs of the Barbary coast. They were well armed with thirty long guns (24 pounders) and twenty 32 or 42-pounder carronades, so that she would have been more than a match for *Desirée* in a single-ship action. [108]

An interesting recording in the Captain's Log (ADM 51/2262) is that while on patrol off the Dutch coast and to and fro over the North Sea, a net would be cast over the ship's side to trawl for fish. Some of her crew may have been East Anglian trawlermen and the addition of fresh fish would have been a welcome supplement to the normal diet of hard biscuit and salted meat.

Once a month the *Articles of War,* which formed the legal basis for naval discipline, would have been read out by the Captain. Drunkenness, probably due to boredom, theft and insubordination were the usual causes of crimes, for which as many as 24 to 36 lashes were inflicted by the bosun's mates, but mainly discipline seems to have been good. By the middle of January she was back in Yarmouth Roads for a few days before being ordered to sail south for a short refit at Sheerness dockyard. Following this she returned to her usual duties of working in and out of Yarmouth and Lowestoft on patrol off the Dutch coast. The only excitement to disturb this routine occurred when, infrequently, enemy ships tried to emerge from behind the Texel; then shots would be exchanged before the Dutch vessels retired. Forbes may have gleaned from his fellow-officers in the wardroom that this blockade of "the Texel" had started in 1795, when the North Sea Squadron had been commanded by Admiral Duncan. In spite of the mutiny at the Nore in 1797, when he had maintained it almost on his own in his flagship *Venerable,* it later became so effective that Dutch trade came nearly to a standstill. Additionally, the amphibious expedition against the Dutch at the Helder in 1799, which resulted in the capture of 12 ships of the line and 13 Dutch East Indiamen without a shot being fired by Duncan, had effectively destroyed or bottled up the Dutch fleet. [109]

Napoleon invaded Russia on 13th June 1812; on the 22nd July Wellington decisively defeated the French under Marshal Marmont (1774-1852) at Salamanca in Spain. The end of the year saw *Desirée* and Surgeon Forbes returning to Spithead via Yarmouth for replenishment of stores.

At Portsmouth *Desirée* took on board fresh provisions and ammunition. With the help of the Dockyard 'mateys', some repairs to the ship were made and the Ship's Company received twelve months' pay. This would have been a notable event and

Forbes may well have celebrated by a good 'run ashore' to visit some of the numerous inns and taverns, for which Portsmouth was famous. Although abstemious in later life, he could have been nursing a 'hang-over' when his ship sailed down the English Channel, encountering its choppy seas, which made *Desirée* pitch and roll, before wallowing in the Atlantic swell of the Bay of Biscay. The destination was Madeira, which was reached in early April without incident. On her return voyage, she captured two American ships - the war with the United States having started in the previous year - and put prize crews aboard to sail them back to England. Surgeon Forbes would have been entitled to a share of the 'prize money' ["The traditional balm to the wounded naval spirit" (Rodger, 2004)], when his ship returned to Spithead in mid-May.

She was back on patrol off the Texel during early July, when some of the gunboats of the squadron came alongside to have rigging repaired and to take on some guns. [Gunboats were ideal for coastal waters as they had a shallow draught. They were armed with two 18-pounders on slides in the bows and another, deployed on a pivot, in the stern. [110] The latter could be replaced by a carronade firing 12-pounder cannon balls at close range. The best had been designed by Commissioner Hamilton in 1805.]

Desirée next sailed to the island of Heligoland off the mouth of the river Elbe, where a small victualling station had been established after its capture from the Danes in 1807. [111] On 7th July the Captain's Log recorded: "fired a Royal salute of 21 guns in honour of Lord Wellington's Victory in Spain". This, almost certainly, refers to the battle of Vitoria, in northern Spain, between Burgos and Bilbao. With the assurance of good supplies by virtue of British sea power, Wellington's army had been able to fight its way out of Portugal and advance towards the port of Santander, which had been captured by a British naval force under Sir Home Popham. [112] On the 13th June, Wellington's 80,000 men decisively defeated King Joseph Bonaparte at Vitoria and opened the way for the complete clearance of all French forces from the Iberian Peninsula. Although John Forbes and his shipmates may not have fully understood at the time, the hour of the Emperor's final defeat was fast approaching. By the end of June, Wellington had reached the river Bidassoa between northern Spain and southwest France but his army was temporarily halted by Napoleon's Marshal Soult and the stubborn resistance of French garrisons at Pamplona inland and San Sebastian on the coast.

Meanwhile, off the mouth of the river Elbe and the north German coast, HMS *Desirée* was preparing for action. A small British force of 32 troops from Heligoland had taken the fortified town of Cuxhaven in March and the brigs, *Blazer* and *Brevdrageren*, had destroyed the French flotilla of 20 gunboats in the harbour. [113] Later, in the same month, the two brigs sailed about 30 miles upstream in the strongly flowing tidal river Elbe, until they found themselves off the Danish port of Brunsbüttel on the east bank of the estuary. In a "very gallant exploit", their crews captured two Danish gunboats with minimal casualties on either side. [114] Unfortunately, Cuxhaven was recaptured by the French, so that the island of Heligoland remained the main base of the Royal Navy off the German coast.

The following is an extract from the Captain's Log (NA ADM 51/2262) of HMS *Desirée* for the morning of 8th July 1813, describing the action against the enemy forts at the mouth of the river Elbe: "Weighed, tacking as necessary work up the river. Found H.M. Brigs CALLIOPE, SHAMROCK, PIERCER lying in the river. Made sail, squadron in company, cleared ship for action, double shotted the guns. [A mixture of round shot and canister shot - the latter for use against personnel.] 6.25 enemy began firing. [Ships working close inshore were vulnerable to red-hot shot heated in furnaces ashore, which could easily cause fires on a wooden ship; it was too dangerous to return heated shot from a naval warship in this situation.] [115] 6.30 wore ship, up foresail and commenced action, with the squadron, against the enemy's batteries at Cuxhaven, sails, rigging and hull little cut by enemy's shot. Enemy ceased firing great guns, took refuge behind their works and commenced a heavy and well directed fire of musketry upon the squadron. [That the British ships were within musket range indicates how close inshore the squadron had sailed.]

Tacking and wearing as most necessary to bring our broadside to bear upon the enemy. [As *Desirée* was a 40-gun frigate, her commander, Captain Arthur Farquahar, was the senior officer of the squadron; the manoeuvre, in shoal waters, required excellent seamanship.]

7.50 the enemy fired several great guns at the squadron.

8.30 recall signal, anchored out of range of the enemy's shot."

These terse sentences in the Captain's handwriting convey only very little of the tension on board the ships of the squadron under constant fire from the big guns of the forts at Cuxhaven; Farquahar and his tiny force had approached near enough for the only effective fire to be from muskets, had escaped running aground and incurred only minimal structural damage to his ships.

Such close inshore action was risky for a frigate, even with reliable charts for these waters, so it is not surprising that subsequent attacks on the forts were made by gunboats. These shallow draft boats also managed to "detain and send down several of the enemy's vessels" over the next two weeks.

During August *Desirée* stayed off Heligoland or at the mouth of the Elbe keeping an eye on the gunboats in action against the Cuxhaven batteries. Later, at the end of October, she sailed up the Elbe for an important rendezvous. Surgeon John Forbes from *Desirée,* with his knowledge of French and German, was sent ashore with despatches for a Russian general at Bremen. [116] The war with France had reached the stage that Crown Prince Bernadotte (1763-1844) of Sweden, formerly one of Napoleon's marshals, was encamped at Berlin with 100,000 Swedish and Russian soldiers. [117] Ironically, Bernadotte's wife was named '*Desirée*', who was once described by Bonaparte as his 'first love'. [118]

According to Parkes' *Memoir* (1862), there is proof of the following incident in a letter, "still extant". The Russian general at Bremen commanded a force of 10,000 Cossacks, whose ferocity was well known to the Scottish naval surgeon. On arrival on shore he was surprised by their courtesy to him; by contrast when they encountered any Frenchmen, "they suddenly seemed possessed with a devil". His escort of ten Cossacks took two French gendarmes by surprise and immediately hacked them to pieces. Forbes' efforts to save them provoked a very hostile response so he had to desist. The bodies of the unfortunate Frenchmen were stripped of their clothing and valuables, whereupon the Cossacks "returned to their previous state of friendliness and good temper" as if nothing had happened!

Parkes' *Memoir* continues (p 15) with a description of how Forbes nearly drowned in an attempt to rescue a sailor "who had been washed overboard" into the strong current of the Elbe. Forbes "was carried down two miles from the ship before he was picked up". Perusals of the Captain's Log (ADM 51/2263) and surviving letters of Captain Farquahar (ADM 1/1810) have failed to reveal any mention of this episode. It is possible that the Captain was very annoyed at seeing his valuable Surgeon leaping overboard in a futile attempt at rescue, thereby upsetting his ship's normal duties and wasting time on a further rescue down river. Was Farquahar so upset that he failed to record it in the Log? The only oblique reference that we have found is in the entry for 'Sept 30':

"Found missing William Oliver, Boy, supposed to have fallen overboard at 12 [noon]".

On October 7:

"Sold at the mast [as was customary] the effects of William Oliver, drowned". The kit of other seamen, who had been killed in recent skirmishes with the enemy, was also sold off.

Other Log entries and dates are: Sept.1: "picked up a dead man and buried him".

Sept.4: "Surgeon and wounded men" sent to Heligoland, which means that there must have been some basic naval sick quarters on the island.

Saturday Sept.10: "received the intelligence of the taking of St.Sebastian and Lord Wellington defeating the French Army in Spain, fired a Royal Salute and dressed the ship in Colours". The capture of the northern Spanish ports of Santander and San Sebastian resulted in Wellington's army being assured of supplies to enable the invasion of southern France to take place and the setting up of a "second front". [119]

October 27: "Captain and Surgeon [Forbes] went in the barge onboard the Wrangler [? small brig or sloop] to the Weser". [Bremen lies on the river Weser]. This was the occasion that Forbes met the Russian general. Certainly, the date is significant: the battle of Leipzig in Saxony had lasted four days from the 16th to the 19th October, when Napoleon's army, outnumbered by those of Austria, Prussia, Sweden and Russia, was decisively defeated. [120] The French were then forced to retreat to the west of the Rhine.

The position of the French garrison at Cuxhaven became hopeless but they fought on bravely until 30th November, when the Captain's Log records laconically "batteries surrendered". The following day, the French Commandant and his officers came on board *Desirée* as prisoners of war.

On the 15th December, HRH the Duke of Cambridge visited the frigate for the day. He was entertained on board and saluted by the firing of "2 guns". [He was the first Duke, Adolphus Frederick (1774-1850), seventh son of King George III (1738-1820)]. Surgeon Forbes would have been presented to HRH with the other officers in the wardroom; this chance meeting later bore fruit, when Dr John Forbes was appointed as Physician-in-Ordinary to the Duke in 1831.

There is another memoir of Forbes' naval career - not recorded in the Captain's Log - mentioned by Parkes (p 15):"It was in the North Sea that Forbes volunteered for a cutting-out expedition; the lieutenant in command showed the white feather, and would not bring the boat within the reach of shot. Forbes, who was all ardour and courage, was so indignant that he tore off his cutlass, and throwing it down at the bottom of the boat, with some strong expressions, declared that he would not be caught on a fool's errand again". See Roger NAM. *The Command Of The Ocean,* London (2004), p.527.

This display of temper, especially in front of the boat's crew, would not have endeared him to his fellow officers and Captain. Surgeons had no executive authority and were barely tolerated in the wardroom. On the other hand, the lieutenant may have had a reputation for being over-cautious and the popularity of the young Scottish surgeon may have soared! Who can tell?

To return to the attack on Cuxhaven on 30th November: James' account is more enlightening than the Captain's Log of *Desirée.* Having established that Farquahar had been placed in command of the British naval force at Heligoland in October, James goes on to say that on that date: "Captain Farquahar...with a small squadron of gun-brigs and gun-boats, successfully co-operated with a Russian force in an attack upon the heavy batteries that defended Cuxhaven". [121]

The next indication of *Desirée*'s activities in the river Elbe is noted in her Captain's Log for Dec.26: "engaged the Danish gunboats and battery at Gluckstart [sic], shore requested the Surgeon". Obviously, by this time, Farquahar's force had ascended much further up the Elbe in an attempt to reduce the Danish fortifications on the right bank of the river. [Denmark was still bravely holding out against the Allies following a declaration of war in 1807.] Gluckstadt was besieged by the Royal Navy on the river and by Crown Prince Bernadotte's Swedish army on land. The town held out for sixteen days, including a bombardment of six days, until surrendering on 5th January 1814. [122]

James mentions that, in addition to the *Desirée* the British squadron included the 10-gun schooner-sloop *Shamrock*, three gun-brigs and eight gunboats with the names of their commanding officers. Captain Farquahar in his despatch singles out for special praise captain Andrew Green, "who commanded a party of seamen and marines on shore". The flotilla's casualties were three men killed and sixteen wounded, including Captain Rose of the brig-sloop *Hearty*, a midshipman and a captain's clerk. Surgeon John Forbes was ordered to go ashore on Boxing Day and was kept busy with the casualties. (The city of Gluckstadt was on fire and one of its magazines had blown up).

By the time the city surrendered on 5th January, *Desirée*'s Log had noted for Dec.30:"Mr Forbes, Surgeon, superceded". The Ship's Muster Log (ADM 37/2537) noted that he was succeeded as Surgeon by Mr Smyttan, while she was in action bombarding the shore batteries. This may appear to be an odd time to be replaced but the reason was, probably, that the cutter HMS *Princess Augusta* had turned up in the river from the island of Heligoland with despatches and also with Forbes' successor as Ship's Surgeon.

Cutters were too small to be used for close inshore bombardment; built for speed, they were single masted, with both fore and aft and square sails. Ideal for carrying despatches, their deep draught ensured that *Princess Augusta* remained out of range of enemy fire in midstream. The term 'cutter' should not be confused with the small ships' boats of the same name used in clandestine 'cutting out' operations.

CHAPTER 12:
BACK TO THE CARIBBEAN

It is unclear how John Forbes returned to England or where he set foot on shore. Certainly, his date of discharge from *Desirée* was '30 December 1813' (ADM 104/30). His ship returned to Spithead via the Nore on 18th January 1814. He may well have returned to Scotland for a couple of months on leave after his adventures in the North Sea and river Elbe. Forbes joined HMS *Benbow* in Yarmouth Roads off the Isle of Wight on 9th March 1814. He is described as a 'Supply Surgeon' i.e. between successive appointments.

[*Benbow* was a Third Rate two-decker of 74 guns. Designed brilliantly by Thomas Slade of Deptford (Surveyor of the Navy between 1755 and 1771), some of these ships were badly built: they were unpopular in the Navy and were nicknamed 'The Forty Thieves'. They were armed with forty 32 pounders 'long guns'; they also carried twelve carronades. A new addition to the Royal Navy, *Benbow* had been launched at Rotherhithe in February 1813 and had a crew of 590 men. Modified from an original French design, the later '74s' were a great success.]

On 10th March *Benbow* set sail for Barbados and arrived on 22nd April (ADM 51/2074). There Surgeon Forbes joined the 74 gun two-decker (Third Rate) HMS *Venerable*. Launched at

Northfleet in 1808 as a replacement for Admiral Duncan's old flagship of the same name, which had foundered in Torbay in 1804, she was well-armed with forty-two 32 pounders, thirty-eight 18 pounders, of which twenty were carronades. She also had a crew of 590. [123]

Unfortunately, Forbes had missed his chance to share in *Venerable*'s prize money, of which he would have earned one-eighth portion of the total value. How this came about was as follows: *Venerable* had sailed from St.Helen's Roads at the Isle of Wight on the morning of 26th December 1813 having on board Rear-Admiral Philip (later, in 1815, Sir Philip) Durham [Fig.16] en route to take command of the Leeward Islands station in the West Indies. On 31st December she captured two small prizes but, on the 16th January 1814, she sighted two French frigates cruising off the Canary Islands. These were identified as the *Iphigénie* and the *Alcmène*, each of 40 guns. They had sailed from Cherbourg the previous October on a six months' voyage as commerce raiders.

This was originally successful but, at 7am on 16th January, their luck ran out when they encountered the *Venerable*. In addition to his 74-gun flagship, Durham had the small 22-gun prize ship *Cyane* and the prize-brig *Jason* under his command with prize crews on board under the command of Captain Thomas Forrest and Lieutenant Thomas Moffat respectively. When the enemy ships separated, the *Cyane* and *Jason* were detached to chase the *Iphigénie* leaving Captain James Andrew Worth in the *Venerable* free to concentrate his fire on Captain Villeneuve in the *Alcmène*. After a brief action, in which the French frigate lost 32 men killed and 50 wounded, including Villeneuve, her colours were hauled down by a British boarding party headed by Captain Worth. British losses amounted to two seamen killed and four wounded.

Meanwhile, the *Jason* had outsailed her consort and bravely engaged the *Iphigénie* with her two small 6-pounder guns at

Figure 16) Admiral Sir Philp Charles Calderwood Durham

Bonhams, Scotland

10pm; it was not until three hours later that she was joined by *Cyane*. She fired three broadsides at the French frigate but soon realized that she was outgunned and withdrew out of range. This was a wise decision in view of the discrepancy in firepower.

Captain Forrest sensibly despatched the *Jason* to search for the flagship, while he continued to chase the French frigate over the course of the next two days and nights until the evening of the 19th January. Captain Emeric of the *Iphigénie* cut away his boats and anchors to try to increase her speed but, at 8am on the morning of the 20th, *Venerable* appeared on the scene and opened fire with her bow-guns. Having fired off her starboard broadside "for form's sake", Emeric struck his colours and surrendered. Both the French frigates were added to the strength of the Royal Navy. [124]

Surgeon Forbes missed this brisk action but, by this time in his career, he had gained an excellent professional reputation. As well as being reliable in the writing of his medical journals, he had the gift of speaking the French language. These attributes were rewarded by his appointment in April as both Flag Surgeon and Secretary to the Commander-in-Chief, Rear-Admiral Durham. Forbes joined *Venerable* on Sunday 24th April 1814, when the flagship was moored in Carlisle Bay, Bridgetown, Barbados. [125]

As Secretary to the Commander-in-Chief of the Leeward Islands station, Forbes would have increased his pay by £300 to £400 but, as "there was a great deal of paperwork involved in running a fleet and most of it was the responsibility of the flag officer's secretary", he would have earned every penny of it. [126]

In addition to dealing with all the Admiral's correspondence he had to "issue orders to individual ships and standing orders to the fleet; he had to supervise the accounts of the standing officers of various ships, and keep a journal of the fleet's movements". Although he was not ranked as Physician-of-the-Fleet

like Blane, Gillespie and Trotter - Forbes did not obtain his Edinburgh medical degree until 1817 - he was required to visit the
ships in the Leeward Islands squadron frequently and to inves-
tigate the health of the crew and the treatment of the sick. He
also acted as chief medical adviser to the Admiral and to his staff
on board the flagship. [127]

While at anchor in Carlisle Bay, carpenters and joiners from
ashore came on board *Venerable* to repair the damage to the sails
and rigging caused in the action with the *Iphigénie* and the
Alcmène. She was also revictualled with 710 lbs. of vegetables,
720 lbs. of fresh beef, which was cut up into 240 pieces, flour,
water and a cask of rum. In addition, 10 cwt. of old canvas and
rope were taken on board, probably to effect running repairs to
the hull at sea. Ammunition for the guns and replacement cables
were also brought on board. At the end of this refit by the
dockyard at Bridgetown, the ship was washed thoroughly,
hammocks were scrubbed and she was painted inside. (ADM
51/2958)

During all this intense activity, Surgeon Forbes would have
had the opportunity to acquaint himself with the flagship's
layout between decks and to introduce himself to the Admiral
and other officers on board. In particular, he would have advised
on any improvements in the standard of hygiene of the ship's
company; this would have been helped by the 'divisional system'
introduced in 1775, whereby the ship's company was divided
into four divisions, each of which was regularly inspected by a
Lieutenant.

There was a weekly muster of clothing, a daily airing of
hammocks and a monthly fumigation by "burning tar or firing
small quantities of gunpowder". [128]

Venerable put to sea on 17th May 1814 in company with two
smaller warships for a short six day voyage around Barbados
during which she could exercise her guns and make sure that

any signals from the flagship were promptly obeyed! She returned to Carlisle Bay on 23rd May for two weeks. She resumed exercising at sea over the next few weeks, which were uneventful. She returned in mid-June but sailed again for the Virgin Islands, where she anchored at St.Thomas on 2nd July.

On the following day she sailed as flagship of a small squadron to escort a convoy bound for England. [British trade in British ships, escorted by the Navy, had been very successful since the introduction of a convoy system in the late 18th and early 19th centuries. In addition, escort commanders had been given legal powers to enforce obedience to their orders.] The presence of a line-of-battle 74-gun ship would have deterred any privateers or enemy warships lurking in the northern Caribbean. By evening on the 3rd July, when well out in the Atlantic, Durham signalled that the convoy should proceed on its own. Patrolling continued with the sighting of 'Strange Sails' recorded in the Log and, in some cases, these unidentified ships were boarded.

Venerable returned to Carlisle Bay on 15th July. The remainder of the year was spent patrolling off the Leewards, including Guadeloupe. [A fatal accident occurred in another ship of the squadron, which Forbes attended. This nearly resulted in a court-martial of the ship's Commanding Officer]. (See Appendix A) The visit to Guadeloupe is of interest in view of the political situation: under the terms of the Treaty of Paris (30th May 1814), in alliance with the European coalition against France, Britain restored to the new French monarchy all her captured colonies in the West Indies except St.Lucia and Tobago. [129] During the war against Napoleon, Britain had promised the island of Guadeloupe - captured in 1810 - to Sweden but, as part of the wheeling and dealing with her other allies (Austria, Prussia and Russia), she now undertook instead to restore the island to France by paying to Sweden the sum of £1,000,000! At the same time, the island of Martinique - captured in 1809 -

was handed back to the French crown. [130] On 23rd November, while at English Harbour, Antigua, *Venerable* embarked Lieutenant General Sir James Leith (1763-1816), commander of the Army for passage to Martinique, where he was landed at Fort Royal five days later. His Excellency and his suite had previously arrived at Barbados, as Governor of the Leeward Islands, on 15th June that year. [131]

HMS *Venerable* seems to have assumed the role of transport over the weeks before Christmas, ferrying troops of the 16th Regiment to St.Lucia on 30th November and Generals McLean, Johnstone and Douglas with 199 men from the 25th Regiment from Basseterre in St.Kitts to English Harbour, Antigua, in December. The Ship's Log does not mention the way in which St.Andrew's Day was celebrated on 30th November but there may have been a piper in the wardroom and a bumper toast to the patron saint honoured in the usual way. This would have been appreciated by the Ship's Surgeon and by any other Scottish officers now fully committed to the Act of Union (1707) between England and Scotland.

The end of the year found *Venerable* at anchor again in Carlisle Bay, Bridgetown. New Year's Day 1815 dawned 'fine with light breezes'. It is worth noting that any naval or military operation in the Caribbean may be influenced by hurricanes at sea and by earthquakes and volcanoes on shore. The latter are occasional hazards but the hurricane season is usually from mid-July to mid-October, although they may occur at other times of the year:

"June, too soon,
July, stand by;
August, you must
Remember September;
October, all over." [132]

This West Indian doggerel may not have appealed to the already mentioned poetic feelings of Forbes but form an apt summary of local weather conditions. They would have figured prominently in the planning by Admiral Durham and General Leith to overcome any indigenous opposition to the restoration of the French West Indian Islands to the Bourbons. Martinique and Marie Galante were retaken without any trouble but it was a different story at Guadeloupe, where the Bonapartists remained in control. [133]

On Sunday 4th June troops from the 25th Regiment were embarked and a Royal salute was fired 'in commemoration of His Majesty's Birthday'. It is interesting to speculate how much this would have affected Surgeon Forbes, who probably had little sense of personal loyalty to the elderly George III; the ailing monarch was prone to bouts of mental illness due to, the then unknown, porphyria. Nevertheless, the British monarchy stood for the principle of liberty as opposed to the tyranny of Napoleon Bonaparte and the King commanded the complete loyalty of all officers and men in the Royal Navy. Forbes would have drunk the 'loyal toast' without hesitation at dinner in the wardroom.

Returning to the Ship's Log (ADM 51/2958): on Sunday 1st January 1815, while at moorings in Carlisle Bay, fresh beef and vegetables were brought on board. The Ship's Company was mustered by Divisions at 1100. During the next few days the sides of the hull were scraped and the crew picked oakum in order to untwist and tease out old tarred ropes so that the Dockyard workers could caulk the seams of the *Venerable*. She resumed normal patrolling duties at sea on 19th January but the Captain George Pringle's Ship's Log records that on the 27th February 'the main top gallant sail split in consequence of it being rotten having been made in 1808 and drawn from the Barbados Yard'. One can picture the ratings swarming up the rigging to the dizzy heights of the maintop to remove the faulty sail and the written broadside from Captain Pringle to the Dockyard Authority! [French sailcloth was of better quality than English].

On 4th June, the day of the Royal salute, a curious incident occurred: a shot having been accidentally left in one of the guns, it fell upon the beach at Gros Islet Bay and severely wounded three persons. As a result of this unfortunate episode of 'friendly fire', *Venerable*'s Gunner was court-martialled and sentenced to be 'severely reprimanded'. Next morning the troops were put ashore at Fort Royal Bay, Martinique.

A change in the 'seventy-four's' command took place on the 23rd July, when Captain John Thomson succeeded Captain Pringle as flag captain. This was unrelated to the accident at Gros Islet Bay and was more likely due to illness or his being due to be relieved at that particular time anyway in order to enjoy a well deserved leave of absence; the Ship's Log does not make it clear.

CHAPTER 13:
THE CAPTURE OF GUADELOUPE IN 1815

We have seen that, under the terms of the Treaty of Paris, all the captured colonies in the West Indies, except Tobago and St.Lucia were restored to French rule. In France, the restoration of the Bourbon monarchy was not generally popular and the Bonapartists plotted the return of the Emperor to the mainland from his exile in Elba. The brief return to power of Napoleon in early 1815, the 'Hundred Days', inspired unrest in several of the French Empire's overseas possessions. Amongst these were the islands of Martinique and Guadeloupe.

The Governor of Martinique, the Comte de Vaugiraud, was loyal to King Louis XVIII. He invited the Governor of Barbados to send British troops ashore in order to prevent any Bonapartist uprising. With the help of the Royal Navy, this took place, unopposed, on 5th June. It was a different story at Guadeloupe, where the Governor was Vice-Admiral the Comte de Linois. As a Rear Admiral in the French Navy, he had been in command during the bloody engagement with Vice-Admiral Sir James Saumarez's squadron in the Bay of Algeciras on 6th July 1801. After hasty repairs at Gibraltar this force, in a confused night action, subsequently routed a numerically superior squadron of French-

Spanish ships a week later. 134 It was not surprising that Linois fully supported the Bonapartists when they raised the tricoleur in Guadeloupe on 18th June, the same day - although they did not know it at the time - as the battle at Waterloo. In response to this insurrection, it was decided by the British and their French monarchist allies to mount an ambitious amphibious operation to regain the island. Troops of the 15th Regiment (Yorkshire East Riding) under the command of His Excellency Sir James Leith were embarked in transports and escorted by Admiral Durham's squadron to the area off Basse Terre at the southern tip of Guadeloupe.

Sir James came from an old Scottish family and, like Forbes, had attended Marischal College at Aberdeen University before joining the British Army in which he had a distinguished career under Wellington in the Peninsular War. This had been rewarded with a knighthood in 1813. Sadly, he was yet another victim of yellow fever in 1816. [131]

Guadeloupe consists of two islands, Grande Terre and Basse Terre, roughly in the shape of a butterfly. A narrow channel less than 100 feet wide separates them. At the present time the island, together with the small islands of Marie Galante, La Désirade and Les Saintes nearby, form a distinct French overseas département like Martinique. [135]

Only five years previously, on 28th January 1810, British troops, including the East Yorkshire Regiment under General Beckwith, had landed at Guadeloupe and forced the French to surrender on the 6th February. [136] However, that amphibious operation had taken place without any threat of a hurricane interfering with the landings. Surgeon John Forbes, along with his naval and military superiors, must have been well aware of the horrendous mortality from yellow fever that had accompanied previous expeditions to the West Indies both on board ships and ashore in the naval hospitals at Barbados, Antigua and

Kingston, Jamaica. Thanks to the medical treatments introduced
by such enlightened physicians as Gillespie and Trotter and the
discouragement by the former of 'blood letting', mortality had
been considerably reduced by 1815. According to Lloyd and
Coulter, citing *Hist. British Army, IV, 496,* the combined losses of
the army and navy between 1793 and 1796 had averaged 35,000
per annum and out of a total of 80,000 sick, about 40,000 died,
"a figure which exceeds Wellington's losses during the whole of
the Peninsular war". [137] Climatic conditions also affected morale
in the Army and Royal Navy; the navy being ever mindful of the
hurricanes which had wrecked the Spanish fleets in October
1780. As preparations were made, these facts must have weighed
heavily in the thoughts of the planners.

The Expedition: 8th-11th August 1815.

This was mainly an assault by the Army; the role of the Navy
being confined to acting as troop carriers and in support
bombardment of the shore defences. The part played by
Venerable as flagship is described by her Commanding Officer's
(John Thomson) Captain's Log. [See Appendix (B)] but two
letters, handwritten by John Forbes as Admiral Durham's
Secretary, describe the build-up to the landings: the first is dated
24 July 1815 and was received at the Admiralty on 12
September. [138] In it the Admiral, having observed '...the
tremendous surf on the island of Guadeloupe and which
continued with heavy rains...' expressed his concern to Sir James
Leith of the dangers '...for an attack of an Island at this period
of the Year'. However, Durham goes on to say that he found the
French governor at Martinique had already assembled a considerable force consisting of all the 'white troops' as well as '...Flat
Bottomed and Mortar Boats' built at his own expense.

113

Moreover, the Comte de Vaugiraud had pressed his argument for an early assault on Guadeloupe by pointing out the strong possibility of the arrival there of '...reinforcements from France'. Durham finished his despatch to the Admiralty by his account of the Council of War held on board *Venerable*: 'Finding His Excellency is resolved to proceed as soon as possible I have offered him the very...disposable Force which will consist of the VENERABLE and four sloops'.

The second letter is from *Venerable* (also written by Forbes) stationed at 'Saintes' off Basse Terre. [139] This informed their Lordships that Durham had sailed from Carlisle Bay at Bridgetown, '...having on board His Excellency Sir James Leith, Major General Sir Charles Shipley, the Heads of the Departments and part of the 15th Regiment [East Yorkshire] in company with the Ships of War, Transports Hired and Bomb Vessels with about Three Thousand Men for this Anchorage, the General Rendezvous, where we shall remain till joined by some detachments from the neighbouring Islands and then proceed against the Island of Guadeloupe'. Durham emphasised 'the danger attending an Expedition at this season with so slender a Force, and such little means there not being a single Flat Bottomed Boat in the Country'. These were a standard part of the equipment of all British amphibious operations. (See *The Command of the Ocean*, by NAM Rodger London (2004); **27**, p.420.) But it was not only the lack of landing craft that worried him, there was also the impending onset of the Hurricane Season in the Caribbean. Durham also seems to have felt isolated, having just recently lost his trusty flag captain, George Pringle, 'who above all other officers and at this time more especially would be of the greatest Service to me being so intimately acquainted with every part of Guadeloupe...' In addition, he seems to have lacked faith in his new French allies: '...I now find myself surrounded by Strangers in whom I place no confidence'. Would he have expressed his fears to his Secretary and, perhaps, asked Forbes to act as liaison officer for which his knowledge of the French tongue could be useful? [The comparison with Eisenhower before the decision to land in Normandy, in spite of the weather on 6th June 1944, is apposite]. In spite of these forebodings of possible disaster, the attack went ahead on 8th August and is described in detail in Durham's despatch to the Admiralty from *Venerable* dated 15 August 1815. [140] 'The last division of the Troops having arrived on the 7th instant, the island having been reconnoitred by the Commander in Chief [Sir James Leith] of the Forces, and myself, aided by that distinguished and indefatigable Engineer Sir Charles Shipley, the Place of debarkation having been determined upon, all Overtures to the Enemy having been rejected with Scorn and the Rainy and Hurricane Season having set in, not a moment was to be lost'. Accordingly, '...I sailed on the 8th instant having onboard the 15th Regiment in company with the Vessels of War and Troop Ships, DASHER, FAIRY, ESPIEGLE, COLUMBIA, BARBADOES, MUROS, CHANTICLEER, FOX (ts), NIOBE (ts), 53 Sail of Transport and Hired Vessels with 5000 Men, a Corp [sic] of Artillery and the usual appendages to the Army and proceeded to the weathermost landing place [at] Sainte Sauveur (it had been proposed to have landed in three divisions at the same time, but the want of Boats put that out of our power) where from the admirable position taken up by Lieutenant George Tupman, Acting Captain of the CHANTICLEER who swept the beach of the few Troops being covered by the FAIRY and ESPIEGLE the debarkation was soon effected. We then dropt [sic] down to the next landing place Grand Auce where we found a large body of Troops and a Battery commanded by Comte de Linois and General Boyer. I ordered Captain Baker of the FAIRY, Captain Chads of the COLUMBIA and Captain Fleming of the BARBADOES to cover the landing of the Troops [and] from their well directed fire, the Battery was soon silenced and the enemy drove [sic] back to a respectable distance. 2000 men were then landed under the command of their galant [sic] Commander in Chief, without the loss of a Man being now dark and late and the Boats not yet returned I postponed the third landing until the following morning when it was accomplished with equal success on the lee part of the Island near Bailliff under cover of the COLUMBIA, CHANTICLEER and MUROS in the face of a very large Force who retreated to the Heights and there capitulated on the morning of the 10th Inst.'.

This letter or despatch was probably dictated to John Forbes as the Admiral's secretary on board *Venerable,* which could account for the vagaries of spelling and punctuation: it is a model of communication to The Lord's Commissioners of the Admiralty at the conclusion of a decisive joint operation: credit should be given to the sound basic education that Surgeon/Secretary John Forbes had received in rural Scotland. Clearly, Durham got on well with Sir James Leith; the fact that Forbes was also a Scot and fellow graduate of Marischal College, Aberdeen, may have played an important part in establishing a harmonious inter-service relationship. In the past, antipathy between Admirals and Generals had been, not uncommonly, a feature of combined operations. [141] Finally, with his letter of 15th August, Durham enclosed a copy of the Terms of Surrender and expressed his admiration for the gallantry of the soldiers in the face of the enemy and commended Sir James Leith for the general plan of attack.

The Country, he felt, should be indebted to the C-in-C, whom he had entertained on board the flagship, for '...his Zeal, Ability and Indefatigable Exertions in forwarding the King's Service'. [The British government presented Sir James with a sword, valued at two thousand guineas; he was created a G.C.B on 2nd January 1816, the year of his death from yellow fever at Barbados in October] [142]

Admiral Durham also was gracious enough to mention '...the great exertions and Fatigues which the Officers, Seamen and Marines of this small Squadron have experienced in collecting, embarking and disembarking Troops etc.etc. but I can assure their Lordships that every Man most cheerfully exerted himself to his utmost and I beg leave to recommend them to their Lordships notice, the Captains employed on this Service are all Commanders'.

This was a broad hint that promotions were due, especially in the imminent 'run down' of the Navy following the end of the War. He put in a good word for his First Lieutenant, Lieutenant Parr, who had been in the flagship with him during the whole of the commission.

Finally, the Comte de Vaugiraud is thanked for sending '...two corvettes and a Schooner [named in the margin] with Troops from Martinique'. The letter is addressed to JW Croker Esq., Secretary to the Admiralty and reached him on the 12th September. It must have caused much pleasure, especially as so much of the cost of fitting out the expedition seems to have been borne by the Comte de Vaugiraud! Interestingly, Durham - perhaps more than Forbes - could speak fluent French, having spent two years in that country before the Wars '...learning the language and mixing freely in society'. [143]

The last letter, written by Forbes on behalf of Rear Admiral Durham, is dated 16th August 1815 and refers to the Prisoners of War: he suggests that they should be sent to France in order to be dealt with by the Duke of Wellington. 'I shall in a few days send them under convoy of FOX to Havre calling at St.Helens for their Lordships orders incase [sic] the Duke should be in England'. [144] For further details of the capture of Guadeloupe in August 1815 and the parts played by the Comte De Linois and his second in command, Baron Boyer De Peyrelean (1774-1856), the reader is referred to 'The Capture of Guadeloupe in

1815' by Denis Haggard in *Journ Soc Army Hist Research*, XIV, (winter 1935), 231-232.

Note: John Forbes would have been entitled to the award of the Naval General Service Medal (NGS) but there is no record of this; the fact is referred to in an article in the *Nelson Dispatch*, 12, Part II, (summer 2017), pp. 695-697 by Peter Clayton.

CHAPTER 14:
EPILOGUE

The victory at Guadeloupe was the first time that Anglo-French co-operation had been tested in the 19th century. In terms of casualties it must be rated only as a skirmish - the British army lost 16 killed and about 50 wounded. Under the terms of surrender, the Comte de Linois and his adjutant-general Boyer were sent back to France. [145] Durham was promoted to Vice-Admiral on 12 August 1819 and to full Admiral on 22 July 1830. In November 1830 he was created GCB; he became an MP for Devizes from 1834 to 1836. He flew his flag as Commander in Chief, Portsmouth, from March 1836 until his retirement from the Navy three years later. He died at Naples in April 1845. [146]

John Forbes continued his duties as Durham's Flag Surgeon and Secretary on the Leewards Islands station until *Venerable* sailed home from Carlisle Bay on Sunday 10th March 1816. The voyage back from the Caribbean to Spithead (Portsmouth), where she arrived on Monday 15th April, was uneventful. [147] After HMS *Venerable* was decommissioned and her crew 'paid off', Forbes was discharged from the Royal Navy on 30th May 1816. [148] He was then placed on the Retired List on 'half pay'. He remained on the Retired List until his pay was commuted by the Admiralty in a circular dated 17th July 1838. [149]

Forbes graduated MD at Edinburgh in 1817 and dedicated his thesis in flattering terms to 'Philip Charles Durham'. While a Physician at Penzance, Cornwall (1817-1822), he achieved universal medical fame by translating into English the classical work on Diseases of the Chest by the French physician René Laënnec. [150] This translation introduced English-speaking readers for the first time to a description of the physical signs heard by listening to the chest using the stethoscope recently invented by the Parisian physician in 1816. Laënnec's discovery and Forbes' translations were vital links in the advancement of clinical medicine from an empiric art to a rational science.

The Scottish physician later practised at Chichester, Sussex from 1822 to 1840 before moving to London. Elected a Fellow of the Royal Society in 1829, [Fig.17] he combined the careers of medical journalism with his duties as a Consulting Physician. Dr Forbes was appointed as Physician to the Court of Queen Victoria in 1841, who knighted him for his services in 1853. He was the author of numerous medical and scientific publications and editor of prestigious British medical journals. His achievements were honoured both at home and abroad by the award of honorary degrees of renowned academic societies in Europe and America.

Sir John Forbes MD, FRCP, FRS, DCL died on the 13th November 1861 at the home of his only son, Alexander Clark Forbes (1824-1901), at Whitchurch-on-Thames just before his seventy-fourth birthday. [151] From his humble origins in the Scottish countryside he had survived the rigours of the Napoleonic Wars in the Royal Navy and attained fame and fortune in the medical profession. In the words of Julian Grenfell (1888-1915), who was killed in battle in World War I: (See p.15)

'The fighting man shall from the sun
Take warmth, and life from the glowing earth;
Speed with the light-foot winds to run,
And with the trees to newer birth;
And find, when fighting shall be done,
Great rest, and fulness after dearth'.

A memorial plaque in Whitchurch Parish Church, placed by Alexander Clark Forbes, describes his late father's personality in glowing terms of filial devotion. [Fig.18] No one would disagree with his conclusion that Sir John Forbes "...died as he had lived, an honour to his noble profession".

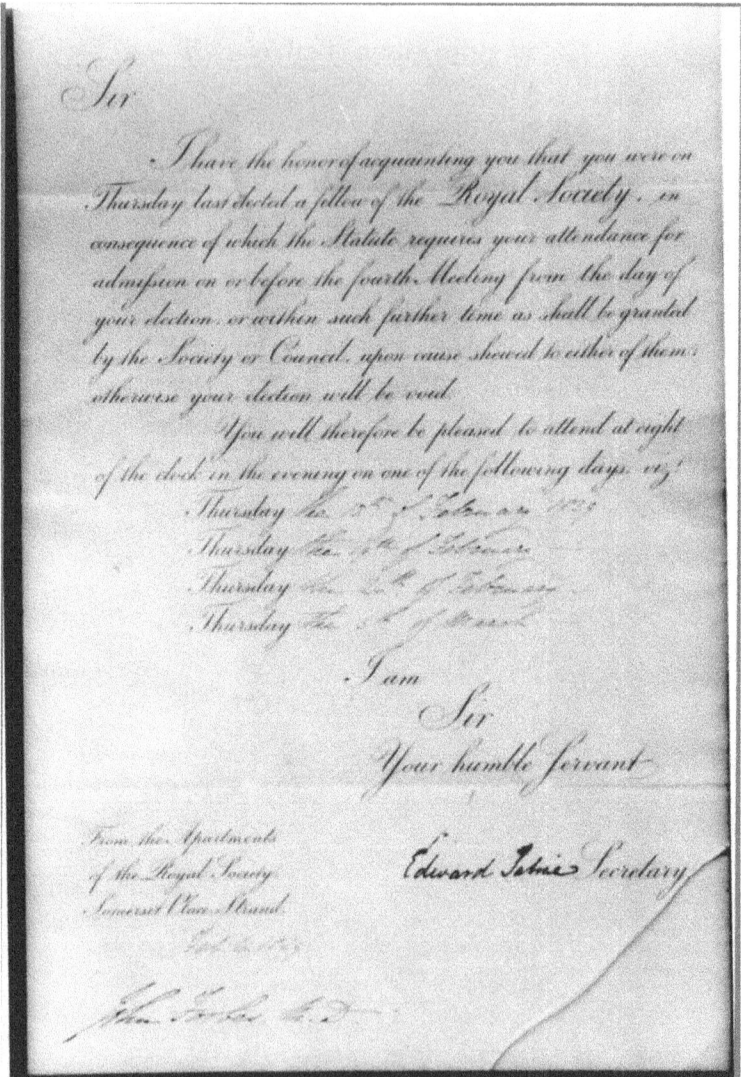

Figure 17) Letter appointing Dr John Forbes a Fellow
of the Royal Society (London)

Forbes Family

Sir
I have the honor of acquainting you that you were on
Thursday last elected a fellow of the Royal Society, in
consequence of which the Statute requires your attendance for
admission on or before the fourth Meeting from the day of
your election, or within such further time as shall be granted
by the Society or Council, upon cause shewed to either of them,
otherwise your election will be void.
You will therefore be pleased to attend at eight
of the clock in the evening on one of the following days, viz.
Thursday the 12th of February 1829
Thursday the 19th of February
Thursday the 26th of February
Thursday the 5th of March

I am
Sir
Your humble Servant

From the Apartments
of the Royal Society   *Edward Sabine Secretary*
Somerset Place Strand
Feb 6 1829

John Forbes M. D.

A facsimile of John Forbes' letter of appointment to the Royal
Society, the original of which appears opposite.

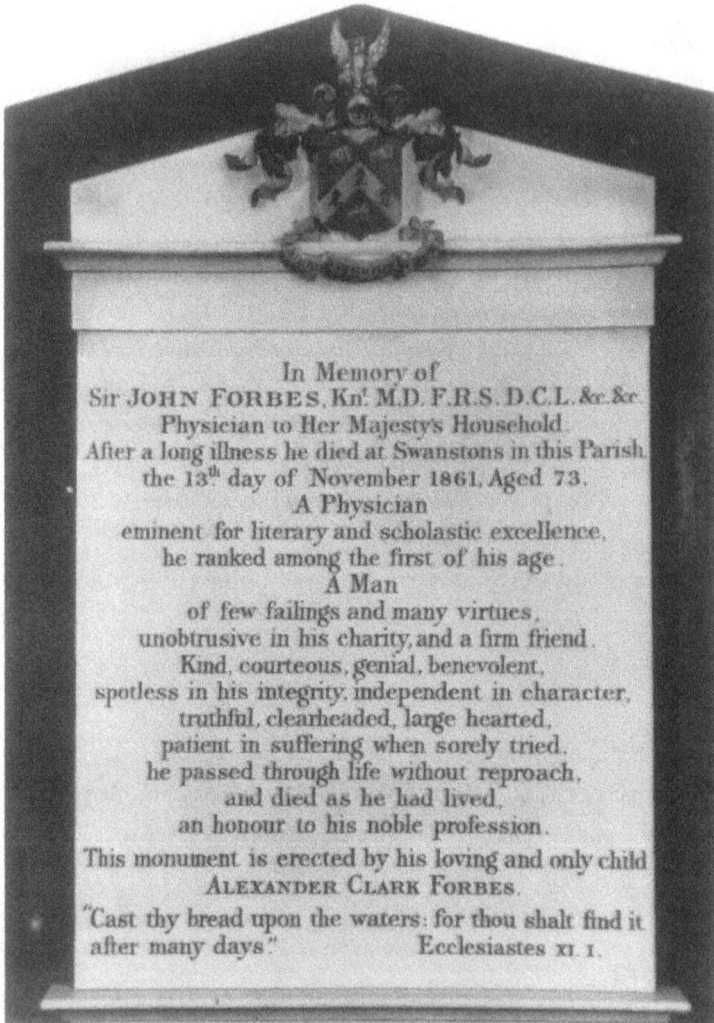

Figure 18) Memorial plaque of Sir John Forbes in
Whitchurch Parish Church.

APPENDIX (A):

In July/August (exact date illegible) 1814, Surgeon John Forbes was summoned from the flagship to attend a badly injured and unconscious young midshipman named 'Keane'. The lad had fallen from the main top of HM Brig *Swaggerer* during the early hours of the morning. Unfortunately, the youth was beyond medical aid and his head injury proved fatal.

One year later, a Board of Enquiry into the accident was held on board the flagship. Surgeon Forbes was required to provide written evidence and his account of the fatality is headed 'HMS VENERABLE, Saintes, August 22 1815':

On examination [of Midshipman Keane] I found there was no fracture of the skull, nor, if I remember right, any external wound; but the symptoms of injury within the skull were so strongly marked as to occasion my mind, great doubts of the Patient's recovery'. [152]

From the evidence it is clear that Midshipman Keane had been sent aloft to the masthead as punishment for 'having been found off deck in Bed in his Watch'. The poor lad had wrapped himself around in his blanket to keep warm during the night and 'rolled himself over the edge of the Top'. The purpose of Forbes' written evidence was to establish the cause of death and vindicate the action of *Swaggerer's* Commanding Officer, Lieu-tenant Alex. Sandilands, in ordering the punishment. Apparently this was successful as Sandilands was not court-martialled, presumably because the Board felt 'mastheading' was a common punishment for erring midshipmen and the cause of death was accidental.

Another letter written from *Venerable* is headed: 'Pursuant to an Order from Sir P.C. Durham KCB, Rear Admiral of the Red and Commander in Chief'. It refers to a Survey and Invaliding Board held at the Royal Naval Hospital, Barbados on 8th July 1815 i.e. just prior to the expedition against Guadeloupe. Of the total of seven ratings seen by the Board, two were from *Venerable* with a diagnosis of *consumption;* both were recommended a 'change of climate'. Other diagnoses included *Maniac, General Debility, Fractured Arm,* and *Rheumatism.* [153]

These two letters, reveal contrasting episodes in the naval career of John Forbes, which varied between action and boredom.

There is no doubt that the Navy made him a better physician well able to distinguish the genuine from the malingerer.

Later, as editor of the *British and Foreign Medical Review* for eleven years between 1836 and 1847, Forbes was ridiculed by the *Lancet* for appearing to support the views of Samuel Hahnemann (1755-1843) on homeopathy as opposed to allopathy. He was also curious about other unorthodox medical movements such as phrenology and mesmerism. As the late Roy Porter has remarked in relationship to the early-Victorian era: "Each [movement] offered a new plan of life based upon Nature's way and claimed to use more natural modes of healing - drawing upon herbs alone, or pure water, or (as with home-opathy) infinitesimal quantities of the purest drugs". [154]

To his credit, Forbes kept an open mind on these subjects but wisely scorned any form of medical humbug.

APPENDIX (B)
SHIP'S LOG HMS VENERABLE (NA ADM 51/2958)

MONDAY AUGUST 7 1815:

'Moderate and cloudy weather'. VENERABLE took on board 'three pounds of fresh beef'. The crew were employed 'fitting and preparing Gun Boats for Service'. With the arrival of HMS CHANTICLEER [18 gun sloop], six casks of Port...one cask of Rum 115 gallons...but in consequence of Leakage, only contains 50 gallons. They also took on board fresh water. At 8 some of the Transports...down to the lower anchorage'. 'Light Airs and variable Southerly'.

TUESDAY AUGUST 8:

'Light Airs and fine weather'. '...hove to off St.Sauveur's Bay'. Some Boats were sent on shore to disembark troops with the '...Brigs and Gun Boats inshore to cover the landing...disembarking the York Rangers, Sir Charles Shipley ['the indefatigable Engineer'] disembarked, most of the Fleet hove to windward'. Later, Lt. General Sir James Leith and all his Staff were landed at Grand Auce Bay. By evening, the weather had changed to: 'Fresh breezes and squally'.

WEDNESDAY AUGUST 9:

'Fresh breezes and Squally...strong current running to Eastward. At 5 weighed and in company with CHANTI-CLEER...' VENERABLE made sail to the eastward and soon sighted the FOX, MUROS and COLUMBIA with several transports off Basse Terre. The Gun Boats covered the landings on the beaches. The Force came under fire from a battery to the north of Basse Terre including 'several shots at us, wore round and fired several Broadsides with the main Deck Guns and a few lower Deckers. Brigs, Transports etc. in shore landing Troops. At noon light breezes and variable. Observed the French Troops advance on our Troops, firing commenced, joined HM Sloop DASHER...and several sail in company. At 8 fresh Breezes and fine weather, made and shortened sail occasionally'.

THURSDAY AUGUST 10:

'Squally with Rain, Thunder & Lightning'. VENERABLE's position was now off 'Upper Saintes'. She sent ' a Boat on shore with 4 Gun Boats to bring the Men back'. The weather continued to be 'Squally' during the rest of the day and VENERABLE set a course again for Guadeloupe. Marine Holden fell overboard and 'was drowned'. Fort Matilda fired shots at VENERABLE, who '...cleared for action and fired Broadsides at the Fort and town. Observed a flag in the town and sent a Boat on shore. Boat returned and at 3.30 observed the English Troops march into Fort Matilda and hoist the English Jack [sic], the Island having surrendered to the British'. At 4 VENERABLE's position was 3 or 4 miles downweather from the Town of Basse Terre and at 12 'Squally with Rain at times'.

FRIDAY AUGUST 11:

'Squally with Heavy Rain, shortened sail'. Later in the day VENERABLE sailed to the Saintes with 'Whale Rock bearing 1/4 of a mile' and by evening there were 'Light winds with Rain'.

SATURDAY AUGUST 12:

'Moored at upper Saintes'. The Admiral shifted his Flag to HMS FAIRY [18 Gun Brig Sloop] temporarily but it is not clear from the Log for what purpose. Later in the day there were 'Moderate Breezes with Rain at times'. A Royal Salute was fired in commemoration of the 'Prince Regent's Birthday'. The Admiral returned and re-hoisted his Flag. HM Sloop BARBADOES arrived and the final entry is: 'Down Top Gallant and Royal Yards. At 8 Squally with Rain'. Here the Log ends but I suggest we add: 'Audentis Fortuna iuvat'. ('Fortune favours the Brave'). [155] This is the motto of the Yorkshire Regiment dating back to the Battle of Minden in 1759.

PROLOGUE: FURTHER READING.

For an account of the Merchant Navy during WWII: See Roskill SW. *A Merchant Fleet in War. Alfred Holt & Co., 1939-1945.* London: Collins, 1962; *The Battle of the Atlantic, 1941,* V pp 92-134; *January-December 1942,* pp 208-239; *Victory in the Atlantic,* 1943, XII pp 259-278.

For causes of, and early single ship naval actions during, the war with the United States: See James W. *British and French Fleets (1812).* In: The Naval History of Great Britain, from the Declaration of War by France in 1793 to the Accession of George IV. New edition, 1886; London: R Bentley & Son, Vol. V, pp 354-424.

For those unfamiliar with the ways of naval life, especially in a schooner of the Royal Navy in 1793, the first chapter of *Cochrane - the Life and Exploits of a Fighting Captain* by Robert Harvey, London, Constable and Robinson Ltd., paperback edition 2002, pp 3-24 is strongly recommended. Entitled *Mr Midshipman Cochrane,* it explains such items of shipboard life as accommodation, food and drink, punishments and esoteric technical terms e.g. 'watches', 'reefing',' tacking' and 'wearing' of a sailing ship.

For an account of the United Irishmen rebellion and naval engagements: See *The Year of Liberty - The Great Irish Rebellion of*

1798 (ref.2). In December 1796, a great storm had prevented the landing of French troops at Bantry Bay in the southwest of Ireland. One of the chief protagonists in the uprising was Theobold Wolfe Tone, who was a Protestant law graduate of Trinity College Dublin. Undeterred by the failure of his first venture in 1796, he returned with a French general (Hardy) and 2,800 men on board a squadron of warships, which had escaped the Brest blockade, for a further invasion attempt two years later.

On the 12th October 1798, this force was intercepted by the Royal Navy (Rear-Admiral Sir John Warren) off the mouth of Lough Swilly on the northern coast of Ulster; in the ensuing fierce battle, the British captured or destroyed most of the French squadron, taking 2,500 prisoners, including Wolfe Tone (1763-1798). He was taken to Dublin, a city still rejoicing from the news of Nelson's victory at Aboukir Bay on the 1st August. There, Tone was tried for treason and condemned to death by hanging. Rather than face such an ignominious demise, he committed suicide by cutting his throat on 10th November.

For an erudite and comprehensive overview of British naval history from the mid-seventeenth century to the end of the Napoleonic Wars: See Rodger NAM *The Command of the Ocean. A Naval History of Britain, 1649-1815.* London: Penguin Books Ltd., 2004.

CHAPTER 1:
EARLY LIFE and EDUCATION:
FURTHER READING.

On the history of Fordyce and its Academy: See McLean DG. *The History of Fordyce Academy. Life at a Banffshire School 1592-1935.* Banff: The Banffshire Journal Limited, 1936. (Reprinted in 1992 by Christine Urquhart, by kind permission of Mrs W.M. Miller).

On the 'Smith Bursary': *See Mither O The Meal Mist. A Pictorial History of Fordyce* by Christine Urquhart. Printed for private circulation by W Peters & Son Ltd., 16 High Street, Turiff (1990), pp 41-42.

James Clark became Physician-in-Ordinary to Queen Victoria (1819-1901), who created him the first baronet of Tillypronie in 1837. He became a close friend and medical confidant to the Queen and Prince Albert for many years. For Clark's medical career: See Cormack AA. Two Royal Physicians: Sir James Clark, Bart., 1788-1870, Sir John Forbes, 1787-1861: Schoolmates at Fordyce Academy. Reprint from the 'Banffshire Journal', 26th June 1965: 1-46. (No.2 King's College Library, University of Aberdeen). Also: The Roll of the Royal College of Physicians of London, comprising biographical sketches by William Munk, M.D., F.S.A. Fellow of the College etc., etc. Second edition, revised and enlarged, Vol 3, 1801-1825. London, 1878: 222-226.

CHAPTER 2.
FURTHER READING and NOTES.

On naval life up to and including the Napoleonic Wars: See Hattendorf JB. *The Struggle with France 1690-1815.* In: The Oxford Illustrated History of the Royal Navy. Gen.Ed. Hill JR: Cons.Ed. Ranft B. Oxford & New York: Oxford University Press 1995; Chapter 4, pp 80-119.

Also recommended are the fictional narratives of naval life by Forester and O'Brian e.g. *The Young Hornblower* by CS Forester. London: Omnibus edition Michael Joseph 1964; Penguin Books edition 1989.

Leonard Gillespie MD became physician to Nelson from January to August 1805, when he was succeeded by another Ulsterman, Surgeon William Beatty (1773-1842). Gillespie advocated supplying orange and lemon juice to the ships and noted the high incidence of pulmonary consumption (TB) and rheumatism in the fleet. [15] He died in Paris aged 83 and is buried in Père Lachaise cemetery. [16]

Surgeon William Beatty will be forever remembered as Nelson's surgeon, who ministered to him when he was mortally wounded at Trafalgar in 1805. He succeeded Surgeon George Magrath (1775-1857) in December 1804, when the latter was appointed by Nelson in VICTORY to take charge of the Royal Naval Hospital, Gibraltar to help in eradicating an epidemic of yellow fever which had caused widespread mortality there. Magrath was successful in doing this but at the expense of frustrating his personal career as Nelson's flag surgeon. In particular, he missed the opportunity of sharing in the glory of Nelson's victory at Trafalgar and caring for the dying Lord Nelson his patron and personal friend. Nevertheless his further career was highly commended and included the awards of the Order of the Bath and the Naval General Service Medal 1793-1818 with two bars Camperdown (1797) and Copenhagen (1801) as well as two foreign decorations. *See Nelson's Surgeon* by Brockliss, Cardwell and Moss (2005) with Afterword, p.196. Also *Sir George Magrath* (1775-1857) by Dr Robin Agnew, published in two parts in the *Nelson Dispatch*, The Journal of The Nelson Society, (Summer 2015), 12, part 3, pp.175-183 and in the same journal, (Autumn 2015) 12, part 4, pp.210-219

For further reading on the relationship between William Beatty and George Magrath and the Yellow Fever epidemic at Gibraltar. See *Nelson's Surgeon – William Beatty, Naval Medicine, and the Battle of Trafalgar* by Laurence Brockliss, M.John Cardwell, and Michael Moss. First published 2005. First published in paperback 2008, Oxford, Oxford University Press. 'Afterword', p.196.

An epidemic in Philadephia of yellow fever caused a large number of deaths estimated as between four and five thousand men, women and children during the period August and December 1793. A local physician, Dr Benjamin Rush (1745-1813), who was an Edinburgh MD, perhaps over-zealously treated his patients by venesection. See: An American Plague by Murphy J. (New York, 2003), *'The Prince of Bleeders'*; 6, pp.57-65.

For further information on Dr Rush, Professor of Chemistry at Philadelphia see: Booth CC. *'Medical Radicals in the Age of the Enlightenment'*. Journal of Medial Biography 2000; 8: 228-240.

CHAPTER 3.
FURTHER READING and NOTES.

For much of the information on this chapter, I am indebted to WN Boog Watson: See *Four Monopolies and the Surgeons of London and Edinburgh.* Journal of the History of Medicine; July 1970: 311-22.

For the career of Henry Dundas (1742-1811), 1st Viscount Melville and Baron Dunira: See *Chambers Biographical Dictionary.* Gen.Ed. M Magnussen KBE, Asst.Ed. R Goring. 5th Edition (1990) Edinburgh: W & R Chambers Ltd., pp 449-450.

CHAPTER 4.
FURTHER READING and NOTES.

The highlight of Anson's Pacific expedition was his interception of the Spanish 'Manila galleon' on 20th June 1743, which had on board over one million pieces of eight and 35,682 oz of virgin silver. Anson sold his prize at Canton and eventually returned home in his remaining ship, *Centurion,* in June 1744, only 145 of the original 1,300 members of his crews survived. See: *Pride and Prejudice Operations 1715-1744* In: The Command of the Ocean - A Naval History of Britain, 1649-1815 by N.A.M. Rodger, London 2004: Penguin Books Ltd., chapter 15: p 239.

See also: Watt J. John Woodall 1570-1643. In: *Notable Barber Surgeons;* The Worshipful Company of Barbers, London (2008) 9, 153-177. 'He [Woodall] was the first to provide an unequivocal clinical description of scurvy and its prevention and cure by lemon juice. To his credit, he prevented he loss of thousands of lives by ensuring that ships of the East India Company carried bottles of lemon juice on sailing from England. P174' Nathaniel Hulme (1732-1807) MD Edin. (1765) was also an early advocate of lemon juice.

Quintessential reading for all information on naval medicine: See *Medicine and the Navy 1200-1900* by C Lloyd & JLS Coulter, Edinburgh & London 1961: E & S Livingstone Ltd. in four volumes. Volume III, Section IV *Sea Diseases,* chapter 18: pp 293-328, deals with the history of scurvy.

Also, strongly recommended is: *A History of Scurvy and Vitamin C* by KJ Carpenter, Cambridge University Press 1986.

For an alternative excellent history of scurvy: See David I Hardie's Introduction to: Limeys - *The True Story of One Man's War against Ignorance, the Establishment and the Deadly Scurvy,* Stroud Glos., Sutton Publishing Limited 2002: pp 1-8. This book details early crude attempts to prevent the disease and later events after James Lind's seminal discovery of a specific remedy. There is a comprehensive bibliography on pp 302-08.

For information on James Cook's (1728-1779) voyages in the Pacific Ocean (1766-1769) and his uncertainty about the aetiology and treatment of scurvy, quoting Sir James Watt's comment on Cook's 'blunderbuss approach': See *The Pacific: Exploration and Exploitation* by Glendyr Williams. In: The Oxford Illustrated History of the British Empire. Editor-in-Chief Wm. Roger Louis. Vol. II, The Eighteenth Century. Editor PJ Marshall, Assistant Editor Alaine Low. Oxford & New York: Oxford University Press 1998; chapter 25, pp 564-65.

Nelson's prayer, written on the morning of the Battle of

Trafalgar, includes the following wish: "..and may humanity after victory be the predominant feature of the British Fleet".

The supposition that Nelson death was suicidal has been disproved by Dr A-M Hills in her book: Nelson – *A Medical Casebook,* Stroud 2006, Spellmount Limited; Chapter IX: 'Refuting suicide and Nelson's religion'. pp. 159-165. She argues convincingly that Nelson's Unitarian beliefs were incompatible with courting death by suicide but concedes that he was a fatalist, putting his destiny in the hands of God in a prayer on the morning of his famous victory.

CHAPTER 5.
FURTHER READING AND NOTES.

The name *Forbes* may have originated from an ancient Scottish legend that the young son of Alexander Bois of Castle Urquhart, who survived the massacre of 1303, killed a fierce bear and thus acquired the appellation of *For-Beast*. This became corrupted to the pronunciation of *Forbes* and, on receiving the accolade of knighthood by King Robert the Second, Sir John Forbes was granted a Coat of Arms showing three bears' heads and a family motto: *Fax mentis incendium gloriae.* See *Historic Irish Mansions No. 28: Castle Forbes, Co. Longford. Seat of the Earl of Granard* by James Fleming. In: *The Weekly Irish Times, Saturday, November 14, 1936,*pp 15-16.

For invaluable information on the 'Forbes of Corse and Craigivar', including a description of the family Coat of Arms (pp 27-8): See *Memoirs of The Earls of Granard* by Admiral The Hon. John Forbes. Edited by George-Arthur-Hastings, Earl of Granard, K.P., London: Longmans, Green, Reader, and Dyer. Dublin: McGlashan and Gill. 1868.

In particular, the reasons why the 2nd Earl, Arthur (1656-1734) remaining loyal to King James II and refusing all bribes from the new King William - who sent him to the Tower of London twice in the 1690s - are explained (pp 72-76). On his release in 1696, he had the misfortune, on returning to his estates in Co. Longford, to find that he was almost bankrupt as a result of the dishonesty of the steward whom he had left in charge. Later, in 1717, he made over the partially restored estate to his son, Lord George Forbes, in exchange for an annuity under generous terms from the 3rd Earl. He died on the 24th August 1734 and was buried at Castle Forbes (pp 78-80).

For an account of the political, religious, economic and demographic changes in Ireland following the Cromwellian wars: See RF Foster. *Restoration Ireland*. In: Modern Ireland 1600-1972, London: Allen Lane - The Penguin Press, 1988; chapter six, pp 117-137.

For the lineage of the Scottish 'Forbes' and the derivation of the surname: See Burke's *Peerage and Baronetage* (1906), p 744. For the Irish 'Forbes': See *Genealogical and Heraldic History of the Landed Gentry of Ireland* by Sir Bernard Burke, C.B., LL.D., 9th edition, London: Harrison & Sons, 1899.

Sir Arthur Forbes (c 1569-1632) became 'Baronet of Nova Scotia' in 1628. He was one of 107 Scottish 'Principal Knights and Esquires', who purchased the title from King Charles I of England, who had created it in 1625 in order to raise money. (Personal communication, Mr N Edelin of the Clan Forbes Society in the USA, quoting *The Highlander, the Magazine of Scottish Heritage*, 34, 1996: pp 1-10).

For further information on the Imperial Russian Court and the role of Anna of Courland: See SS Montefiore. *Prince of Princes - The Life of Potemkin*. Part one: Potemkin and Catherine 1739-1762. *The Provincial Boy*. London: Phoenix Press, paperback edition 2001; pp 27-28.

CHAPTER 6.
FURTHER READING and NOTES.

On the life and career of Dr James Johnson (1777-1845): See
Dictionary of National Biography (DNB) 10, pp 904-05 and the
London Medical Directory 1846, pp 185-87. Following a four
year voyage in HMS *Caroline* to India and China, he published
(1807) an account of this entitled *The Oriental Voyager*; in 1938,
this was extracted by Surgeon Lieutenant-Commander S. Jenk-
inson, Royal Navy, and published in the *Journal of the Royal
Naval Medical Service,* Vol.24 1938, 179-183.

Johnson made some sensible suggestions for the improvement
of the health of British seamen, especially as regards to general
hygiene. He was present at the disastrous expedition to capture
the island of Walcheren in 1809, where he contracted 'fever'
(probably malaria), which decimated the attacking British forces.
In 1812, Johnson published *The Influence of Tropical Climates on
European Constitutions,* which was based on his own experience
in the East. After his retirement from the Navy, he was editor of
the *Medico-Chirurgical Review* and physician extraordinary to
William IV (1765-1837), 'the sailor king'. His career in medical
journalism lasted until his death in 1845.

Robert Melville (1723-1809): See DNB, Vol.XIII 1967-68,
pp 246-47. As an Army major, he commanded the 38th
Regiment of Foot at the capture of Guadeloupe in 1759 and
became Lieutenant Governor of the island. In the same year he
invented the carronade but it was not until 1779 that it was
manufactured for the Navy.

Charles Middleton (1726-1813): See DNB Vol.XIII 1967-68,
p 341. He succeeded Dundas as First Lord of the Admiralty on
30th April 1805 and was created 1st Baron Barham on 1st May.
He was also instrumental in 'copper-bottoming' for the hulls of
the Fleet, which after initial problems was successfully adopted.'

See *'The Command of the Ocean'* (2004) **2** 1649-1815, p.375 by NAM Rodger.

Scurvy in the Channel Fleet in 1806: See Brockliss L, Cardwell J, and Moss M. In: *Nelson's Surgeon Sir William Beatty* (1773-1842). Oxford (2008): Oxford University Press; 5 162.

Sir Gilbert Blane (1749-1834): *See Royal Poxes & Potions* by Raymond Lamont-Brown, Sutton Publishing Limited 2001: Chapter 7, pp 113-14. He retired from the Navy in 1805 and became Physician to the Prince of Wales. When Prince George became Prince Regent in 1811, he made Blane a baronet and his personal physician in 1820. He published his observations on ...*the progressive improvement of the health of the Royal Navy at the end of the eighteenth century and the beginning of the nineteenth century*, London, 1830. He died four years later.

David MacBride (1726-78): See *A Dictionary of Bookplates of Irish Medical Doctors, with short biographies* by Edward A. Martin MD, published by Edmund Burke, Dublin, 2003: pp 82-3.

After an apprenticeship with a local surgeon in Ballymoney, Co. Antrim, he served as a surgeon's mate and studied in Edinburgh and London before settling in medical practice in Dublin in 1761. He published *Experimental Essays* in 1764, which gained him the award of MD Glasgow in the same year. A second edition of Experimental Essays (1767) was in five parts: part 1 was on the digestion of food and fermentation in the digestive system; part 2 on the chemistry of "Fixed Air"; = carbon dioxide; part 3 on the properties of various kinds of antiseptics; part 4 on Scurvy with suggestions for ways of its prevention and cure "at sea"; part 5 on the solvent properties of Quicklime and further studies on "Fixed Air". His ideas on the prevention of scurvy were given an uncontrolled trial by his brother, John MacBride, who was in command of HMS *Jason* on a voyage to the Falkland Islands in 1765-67. Alexander Young, who was the ship's surgeon, forwarded his journal to Dr David MacBride but the results were inconclusive as oranges and apples had been given to the scorbutic seamen at the same time as the infusion of malt. (See: *But the Power is in Others.* In: Limeys - The True Story of One Man's War against Ignorance, the Establishment and the Deadly Scurvy by David I. Harvie, ref 23, pp 123-27).

In 1769 he was elected an honorary member of the Royal Dublin Society for his work on introducing lime water into the tanning industry in Ireland. He also published a textbook on Methodical Introduction to the *Theory and Practice of Physic*, London (1772), which embodied the medical teaching system in Dublin at that time; Latin and French translations duly appeared later.

As Martin (2003) has pointed out, MacBride's medical career was frustrated by his not having a degree from Oxford, Cambridge or Dublin. He died in 1778: his bookplate depicts a crest with ribbon and the motto *Nil Conscire Sibi* (to have a guilt-free conscience).

On the fate of the small French fleet which sailed from Brest to reinforce General Humbert's landing in Co. Mayo in September 1798 See: Rodger NAM. *The Second Coalition - Operations 1797-1802.* In: The Command of the Ocean. A Naval History of Britain, 1649-1815. London: Penguin Books Ltd., 2004; chapter 30, p 457. Essentially, this expedition was "too little, too late". Even so, such threats formed a constant distraction for the Channel Fleet from the Brest blockade. (p 462)

CHAPTER 7.
FURTHER READING AND NOTES.

On the life and naval career of Surgeon Leonard Gillespie (1758-1842), MD St. Andrews (1795): See Keevill JJ. *Bulletin of the History of Medicine* July-August 1954, Vol.28: 4, pp 301-32. He was born in Armagh of Scottish parents, who had migrated to Ulster in the mid-eighteenth century. He studied anatomy and surgery in Dublin before travelling to London, where he passed the examinations at the Company of Surgeons and entered the Navy. He gained extensive experience in naval medicine, especially in the West Indies.

He wrote *Advice on the Preservation of the Health of Seamen in the West Indies* (1798) and *Observations on the Diseases in HM Squadron in the Leeward Islands* (1800), much of which was based on his experience in charge of the naval hospital at Martinique. This work has been summarized in *The diet and health of seamen in the West Indies at the end of the eighteenth century* by TP Gillespie in the Journal of the Royal Naval Medical Service 1951, 37 (4): 187-192.

CHAPTER 8.
FURTHER READING AND NOTES.

Sir Charles Napier (1786-1860) was the eldest son of Captain the Hon. Charles Napier, Royal Navy: See J.K.L. Dictionary of National Biography (Op. cit. ref 34): vol.14, pp 38-45. He joined the Navy in 1799 and was promoted as acting-commander of a brig in 1807 but, within a year: "In August 1808 he was moved to the 18-gun *Recruit*, and in her, on 6 Sept., fought a spirited but indecisive action with the French sloop Diligente. Napier had his thigh broken, but refused to leave the deck till the engagement ended by the fall of the *Recruit's* mainmast. In February 1809 he distinguished himself at the reduction of Martinique; and still more in the capture, on 17 April, of the Hautpolt of 74 guns, which was brought to action by the *Pompée*, mainly by the gallant manner in which the little *Recruit* embarrassed her flight during the three days of the chase". He became

Vice-Admiral in 1853 and Admiral in 1858. He died at Merchistoun Hall, near Portsmouth.

Sir Alexander Forrester Inglis Cochrane (1758-1832) was the younger son of Thomas Cochrane, eighth earl of Dundonald: See J.K.L. Dictionary of National Biography (Op. cit. ref. 34): vol 4, pp 615-16. He joined the Navy at an early age and was wounded in action off Martinique in 1780; commanded the 80-gun *Ajax* supporting landing of troops on the coast of Egypt in 1799. He was appointed commander-in-chief of the Leeward Islands in 1805 and took part in the action off St. Domingo in the 74-gun *Northumberland* as Rear Admiral in 1806 and was knighted. In 1809, he flew his flag in the 98-gun *Neptune,* as we have seen, at the capture of the *D'Hautpolt;* he was naval commander in the combined operation to capture the island of Guadeloupe from the French in January/February 1810. [See W. James, Colonial Expeditions - West Indies. In: *The Naval History of Great Britain;* vol.5, pp 190-91] He was promoted Vice-Admiral in 1809, Admiral in 1819 and died in Paris in 1832.

[He should not be confused with his very courageous but turbulent nephew, Lord Thomas Cochrane (1775-1860), who was involved in the court-martial of Admiral Lord James Gambier (1756-1833) after the Battle of the Aix Roads in April 1809: the incomplete destruction of a French fleet off the mouth of the River Charente had, nevertheless, prevented its sailing to the West Indies, where Martinique and Guadeloupe were soon captured by the British. Later, as Admiral Lord Cochrane he liberated Chile, Peru and Brazil from the Spanish and Portuguese].

During the action off Puerto Rico (p 40), *Castor* opened fire with her 'larboard guns'. This adjective refers to the left-hand or port side of the ship i.e. the opposite to the right-hand or starboard side facing forwards.

'To rake' (p 41) means to fire one's guns down the length of an opposing ship from bow to stern or vice versa, often with devastating effect.

CHAPTER 9.
FURTHER READING AND NOTES.

For an interesting account of the careers of Napoleon and Wellington: See *The Duke and the Emperor* by Major-General John Strawson, published by Constable, London, 1994. Chapter 6, *Peak of Power and a fatal Blunder*, mentions the town of Vimeiro in the Peninsular campaign of Wellington. This little Portuguese town, just north of Lisbon, marked his first victory over the all-conquering French in 1808. Amazingly, the gains were dissipated at the subsequent Convention of Cintra, under the terms of which the French armies and their equipment were allowed to be evacuated and shipped home in transports provided by the British!

Although the spelling of the scene of Wellington's victory differs slightly from the re-named 16-gun brig captured from the French in October of that year, it would have been appropriate for the Navy to have chosen *Vimiera* to replace Pylade.

CHAPTER 10.
FURTHER READING AND NOTES.

For details of the Founding of the naval hospitals at Haslar (1754): See Lloyd C and Coulter JLS (ref.15); chapter 16, pp 207-60 and Plymouth (1760): See The History of the *Royal Naval Hospital, Plymouth* by Surgeon Captain PDG Pugh OBE, FRCS. Reprinted from the *Journal of the Royal Naval Medical Service* vol.58, (1972); pp 78-94.

For the evolution of patient care at Haslar from 1754 to the present day: See Haslar - *The Royal Hospital* by Surgeon Vice-Admiral AL Revell CB, Gosport Society Publications, 2000. The uncertainty of its future as a viable naval hospital (p 46) makes poignant reading for all those with an interest in the future of naval medicine.

For more information on the *Gilbert Blane Medal:* See the detailed article by Surgeon Captain JLS Coulter, Royal Navy in the Autumn (1960) number, *Journal of the Royal Naval Medical Service*, 46(4): 183-191. The winner in 1937 was 'William John Forbes Guild'.

For the life and career of Edmund Alexander Parkes (1819-1876), professor of hygiene and physician: See DNB vol.15, pp 294-96. He graduated MB Lond. in 1841 (Univ. College and Hospital) and his thesis *Remarks on the Dysentery and Hepatitis of India* earned him the degree MD Lond. in 1846. Parkes was editor of the *British & Foreign Medico-Chirurgical Review* from 1852 to 1855. Later, he became professor of hygiene in the new Army Medical School, which was transferred to the Royal Victoria Hospital at Netley in 1863. The following year Parkes published the first edition of his *Manual of Practical Hygiene,* which received widespread acclamation. He was elected a Fellow of the Royal Society in 1861. A man of high achievement in general and preventive medicine, he has been described by *WWW* in the *DNB* as "the founder of the science of modern hygiene".

The anecdotes about Forbes' naval experiences in the Leeward Islands and North Sea Squadron originate from a *Memoir* written by Edmund Parkes in the year after the Scottish physician's death. This was penned at the suggestion of his son, Alexander Clark Forbes (1824-1901). Unfortunately for biographers, John Forbes had burned nearly all his papers some 18 months before he died in 1861. One may therefore surmise that some of what Parkes recorded in his *Memoir* may have become distorted by being passed on by word of mouth rather than by factual evidence in Ships' Logs etc. As in all obituaries, the writer is never "on oath".

CHAPTER 11.
FURTHER READING and NOTES.

The American colonies revolted in 1776 and declared their independence: commissioned as First Lieutenant in the fledgling US Navy, John Paul Jones (1747-1792) raided British waters in his sloop *Ranger* culminating in his victory at the Battle of Flamborough Head in 1779. His career is described by Brian Lavery in *The Conquest of the Ocean,* London (2013),**116**, the Age of Empire 1600-1815, pp.164-172. Jones died in Paris in 1792.

The role of the US Brig *Argus* (Captain AH Allen) as another commerce raider off the coasts of the British Isles has been described by Agnew, RAL in: *Journal of Medical Biography* 2008; **16**: 77-83. During a four month period between May-August 1813, a total of nineteen ships were captured. She was finally caught off St.David's Head in St.Georges Channel by HMS *Pelican.* As the British frigate closed in on *Argus,* her crew lined her sides and gave three cheers for the Americans! Early in the action, Captain Allen was struck by a cannon ball and Surgeon Inderwick (d.1815) had to amputate his leg. After heavy cannon and musket fire at close range Argus, having been boarded, surrendered to *Pelican* and was brought to Plymouth as a prize. There Inderwick attended his Captain, who died after a few days in hospital. The funeral was attended by a Royal Marines band and the coffin was carried by eight captains of the Royal Navy and eight crewmembers of the *Argus.*

For an account of a light boats expedition up the river Elbe to Brunsbüttel in March 1813: See James W. (Op.cit.ref 64): Vol.VI (1859), pp 5-6. Lieutenant Thomas Devon with 8 men from the Brig *Blazer,* including his 12-year-old brother, Midshipman Frederick Devon, bravely captured the Danish gunboat *Jonge-Troutman* on 21st March 1813.

For an explanation of Bonaparte's 'Continental System' of blocking British goods being exported from the "nation of shop-keepers" to the European mainland: See Lewis M. (Op.cit.ref 44): 13, pp 205-6.

CHAPTER 12.
FURTHER READING and NOTES.

On the capture of the *Iphigénie* and *Alcmène*; See James W. (Op.cit.ref.64): Vol.VI, pp 122-23.

For all information on ships of the Royal Navy between the years 1688 and 1855, the reader is referred to The Sailing Navy List by David Lyon, (Op.cit.ref.55). *The Napoleonic War, 74 gun third rates,* vol.7, pp 113-14 refers to the 'Forty Thieves'.

The curious loss of temper by Forbes during the "cutting-out" expedition and its possible consequences as regards his fellow-officers' behaviour on board *Desirée* may be explained by reference to *Honour and Saltbeef. Social History 1793-1815: Officers.* In: The Command of the Ocean. A Naval History of Britain 1649-1815 by N.A.M. Rodger. London: Penguin Books Ltd., chapter 33, p 527.

This points out that Surgeons in the Royal Navy did not receive a proper uniform until 1805 with the addition of a status-giving sword thus leading to 'wardroom rank'.

Rodger has also given a reason for the apparent generosity of Britain's restoration of Martinique and Guadeloupe to France in 1814: it was intended as a gesture to regain a little amour propre for the restored Bourbon monarchy in Paris but without disturbing British commercial interests in the West Indies. (See *No Greater Obligations. Operations 1812-1815.* Chapter 36, p 573).

CHAPTER 13.
FURTHER READING and NOTES.

Note 1: A *Bomb Vessel* or *Bomb* was a small ship of shallow draught, which was used for close inshore bombardment; the main weapon was a mortar, which fired an explosive shell of high trajectory - often with devastating effect.

Note 2: The 15th Foot (Yorkshire East Riding) became the East Yorkshire Regiment in 1881; it was so named until its amalgamation with the West Yorkshire Regiment in 1958 to form the Prince of Wales' Own Regiment of Yorkshire. The Regiment was awarded the battle honour of *Guadeloupe* in recognition of its contribution to the capture of the island from the French in 1810, five years previous to the amphibious operation of 1815.

Note 3: Yellow fever, to which Sir James Leith succumbed in 1816, was the scourge of the West Indies as well as Equatorial Africa. Also known as 'yellow jack' in the Fleet, it carried a high mortality and is transmitted by the bite of the mosquito *Aedes aegypti*. The cause has now been identified as a virus and the main symptoms and signs are fever and jaundice. It was probably carried to the West Indies by African slaves and is best controlled by prevention against mosquito bites and modern vaccination. [See: *The Oxford English Reference* Dictionary, Edited by Pearsall J and Trumble B., second edition, Oxford and New York: Oxford University Press, 1996; p 1676].

Note 4: General Boyer had, as a Major, taken part in the successful recapture by the French of Diamond Rock in June 1805. Situated off the island of Martinque, it had been taken by the British in January 1804 and fortified so that its guns effectively blockaded the approaches to the main French base in the Caribbean. This was a source of "irritation to the French on Martinique and a constant humiliation to the naval administration in France". See *The War For All The Oceans – From Nelson at the Nile to Napoleon at Waterloo.* By Roy and Lesley Adkins, London 2006. Little, Brown Book Group, Chapter 7 'Invasion Fleet' p.132.

Note 5: For further details of the Capture of Guadeloupe in August 1815 and the parts played by the Comte de Linois and his second-in command General Boyer, the reader is referred to an excellent illustrated account entitled 'The last fight for Napoleon, *Journal of the Society for Army Historical Research,* Vol. XIV, No.56 (Winter 1935), pp.231-232 by Denis Haggard.

CHAPTER 14.
FURTHER READING and NOTES.

The Life of Sir John Forbes (1787-1861). by Dr RAL Agnew, Bernard Durnford Publishing, 2002, ISBN 0 9535670 7 9, gives a full narration of this remarkable Victorian physician's life. The book was reviewed in the Journal of Medical Biography November 2002. To quote: "A bonus in this account of an outstanding doctor is a glimpse of the exploits, in the Napoleonic Wars, of ships of the Royal Navy, in some of which Forbes' role exceeded that of a surgeon - more like that of a real-life Hornblower". Hence this attempt, in chronological terms, to describe his naval career in more detail.

Charles-Alexandre-Léon Durand Comte de Linois (1761-1848) was Governor of Guadeloupe from 12th December 1814 until its surrender to the British on 10th August 1815. (British occupation lasted until 25th July 1816). After his defeat by Saumarez at the Straits of Gibraltar in 1801, Rear-Admiral Linois attacked a convoy of East Indiamen in the Malacca Straits in 1804 but failed to press home his assault in spite the advantage in firepower of his French naval squadron over the unescorted and civilian manned Indiamen.

According to his entry in the internet (updated 15th July

2004), which quotes an article in French by Wikipédia in l'encyclopédie libre (http//fr.wikipedia.org//wiki//Charles de Durand-Linois), he was born in Brest on the 27th January 1761 and died at Versailles on 2nd December 1848 aged 87. The greater part of his naval career took place in the Indian Ocean and he lost his left eye when he was gravely wounded at the battle of Groix in 1795 and made prisoner in 1806. He was created an Imperial Count in 1810 and an honorary vice-admiral in 1825.

References for
John Forbes' naval career.

1) Whiting W. 'For those at sea' In: *Songs of Praise*, Words Ed. Dearmer P., Music Eds. Vaughan Williams R., Shaw M. Enlarged edition with music. London: Oxford University Press, twenty-third impression, 1931; p 336.

2) Pakenham T. 'Olive Branch' In: *The Year of Liberty*, London: Weidenfeld & Nicolson, abridged edition 1997; part four, p 97.

3) Craig J. *A general dispensary practice 150 years ago.* Aberdeen University Review, 1972; 44:364.

4) Anderson-Smith M. Personal communication [Mrs Anderson-Smith, Senior Curator Retd., Historic Collections Special Libraries and Archives, King's College, University of Aberdeen].

5) Parkes EA. 'Memoir of Sir John Forbes, Kt.' Reprinted by permission, from the January Number, 1862, of the *British & Foreign Medico-Chirurgical Review* (For Private Circulation). By EA Parkes, with preface by Alexander C Forbes. London: Savill & Edwards, 1862: 8,9.

6) Cormac AA. 'Two Royal Physicians: Sir James Clark,Bart., 1788-1870, Sir John Forbes, 1787-1861: Schoolmates at Fordyce Academy'. Reprint from the *Banffshire Journal,* 26th June 1965; 31.

7) Cormac AA.' An Historic Outline of the GEORGE SMITH BOUNTY (Fordyce Academy). Reprinted in serial form in the *Banffshire Journal* (Dec.4, 1951 - Jan.15, 1952), 18.

8) 'Surgery'. In: *The Oxford English Reference Dictionary,* Eds. Pearsall J and Trumble B. Second edition, 1996; Oxford & New York, Oxford University Press: p 1452.

9) Taylor S. 'John Keats (1795-1821)'. *Journal of Medical Biography,* 1994; 2: 211.

10)Newbolt H.'After Trafalgar'In: *The Year of Trafalgar,* Chapter X; London: John Murray 1905; p 180.

11) Ibid: p 181.

12) Stevenson AM. Personal communication (Miss Alison Stevenson, Archivist of the Royal College of Surgeons of Edinburgh).

13) Public Record Office: ADM 104/30, p 509.

14) Parkes EA.(Op.Cit. ref 5): 9.

15) Lloyd C and Coulter JLS. 'Nelson and the Surgeons' In: *Medicine and the Navy: 1200-1900.*Vol.III 1714-1815. Edinburgh and London 1961: E & S Livingstone Ltd., chapter 12, p 151.

16) Keevill JJ. 'Leonard Gillespie M.D, 1758-1842'. *Bulletin of the History of Medicine1954*; 28: 301.

17) Booth CC. 'Medical Radicals in the Age of Enlightenment' In: *Keith Brown Memorial Lecture,*delivered at the Liverpool Medical Institution on 18th May 2000; 39-40.

18) Watt J. 'Surgeon James Ramsay (1733-1789): the Navy and the slave trade'. *Journal of the Royal Society of Medicine* 1994; 87: 775-76.

19) Watson WN Boog. 'The Guinea Trade and Some of Its Surgeons'. *Journal of the Royal College of Surgeons of Edinburgh* 1969; 14: 213.

20) Lavery B. 'Medicine and Health' In: *Nelson's Navy, the Ships, Men and Organisation 1793-1815.* Part IX - Shipboard Life; London: Conway Maritime Press 1989; p 212.

21) Ibid: 212,213.

22) Ibid: 214.

23) Harvie DI. 'A Learned Man' In: *Limeys-The True Story of One Man's War against Ignorance, the Establishment and the Deadly Scurvy.* Stroud, Glos.: Sutton Publishing Limited 2002; p 76.

24) Watt J. 'The medical bequest of disaster at sea: Commodore Anson's circumnavigation 1740-44'. *Journal of the Royal Naval Medical Service* 1999; 85: 33-39.

25) Baugh DA. 'Health, Victuals, Discipline, and Morale' In: *The Oxford Illustrated History of the Royal Navy.* Gen.Ed. Hill JR:Cons.Ed. Ranft B. Oxford & New York: Oxford University Press 1995; Chapter 5, The Eighteenth-Century Navy as a National Institution, 1690-1815; pp 141-42.

26) Harvie DI. 'Lime Juice and Wine Merchants' In: Limeys-*The True Story of One Man's War against Ignorance, the Establishment and the Deadly Scurvy.* Stroud, Glos: Sutton Publishing Limited 2002; pp 223-24.

27) Lavery B. (op.cit.ref 20): 217.

28) Kennedy L. *The Elite of the Navy of England.* In: Nelson's Band of Brothers. London: Odhams Press Limited 1951; PartII p 96.

29) Ellis H. 'Nelson's Wounds' *Journal of the Royal Naval Medical Service* 1994; 80: 166-68.

30) O'Brian P. In: *Master & Commander.* London: HarperCollins Publishers 1996; Chapter Two: p 38.

31) Kennedy L. (Op.Cit.ref 28): 177-79.

32) Burke B. 'The Granard Lineage'. In: *Burke's Peerage & Baronetage.* London: Burke's Peerage Limited 1876; p 531.

33) *Burke's Peerage, Baronetage and Knightage.* London: Burke's Peerage Limited 1970; 105th edition, p 1153.

34) J.K.L. Forbes, John (1714-1796). In: *Dictionary of National Biography*, eds. Stephen L and Lee S. London: Oxford University Press for Spottiswoode & Co., 1967-1968; 7: 404-405.

35) Debrett. In: *Debrett's Illustrated Peerage. Peerage & Baronetage,* eds. Kidd C and Williamson D. London: Macmillan, 1995; p 489.

36) Lavery B. 'Warrant Officers' In: *Nelson's Navy, the Ships, Men and Organisation 1793-1815*. Part IV - Officers; London: Conway Maritime Press 1989; p 101.

37) Ibid: quoting Lloyd and Coulter. *Medicine and the Navy 1200-1900.* Vol.III, 1961, p 21.

38) Ibid: p 101.

39) Lloyd C and Coulter JLS. 'The Revolution and Napoleonic Wars'. In: *Medicine and the Navy:* 1200-1900. Vol. III 1714-1815; Edinburgh and London 1961: E & S Livingstone Ltd., chapter 13, p 176.

40) Lavery B. 'Ships of the Line' In: *Nelson's Navy, the Ships, Men and Organisation* 1793-1815. Part II - Types of Ships; London: Conway Maritime Press 1989; pp 43-44.

41) Ibid:'Masts, Sails and Rigging'. Part III - Ship Building and Fitting; p 73.

42) Talbott JE. 'The Rise and Fall of the Carronade'. *History To-day* 1989; 39: 25.

43) Baugh DA. 'Ships, Dockyards and Bases'.(Op.Cit. ref 25):p 132.

44) Lewis M. 'The Triumph of the Royal Navy'. In: *The History of the British Navy.* London: Penguin Books Ltd., 1997; chapter 13 The Napoleonic War. pp 198-201.

45) Lloyd C and Coulter JLS. (Op.cit.ref 39): 169.

46) Lewis M. (Op.Cit.ref 44): 139.

47) James W. 'British and French Fleets'. In: *The Naval History of Great Britain from the Declaration of War by France in 1793 to the Accession of George IV.* Vol. IV. A New Edition with Additions and Notes, bringing the Work down to 1827, London: Richard Bentley & Son, 1886; p 196.

48) Ibid: p 231.

49) Ibid: pp 232-33.

50) J.K.L. 'Duckworth, Sir John Thomas (1748-1817)'. (Op.cit.ref 34); 6: 92-95.

51) Clowes WL. 'Major Operations, 1803-1815'. In: *The Royal Navy. A History from the Earliest Times to the Present.* London: Sampson Low, Marston & Co., Vol.V (1900): chapter XXXIX, p 229.

52) NA ADM 51/1642.

53) NA ADM 51/1642, 1781, 2728.

54) NA. ADM 51/1861 & ADM 37/950.

55) Lyon D. The Sailing Navy List: *All the Ships of the Royal Navy- Built, Purchased and Captured, 1688-1855*.London: Conway Maritime Press, 1993; p 39.

56) Ibid: p xiv.

57) NA ADM 51/1999 & ADM 37/1905.

58) Lyon D. (Op.cit.ref.55): p 84.

59) NA ADM 51/1999:Captain's log *Castor* 17 April 1809 & ADM 37/1905: muster/pay book *Castor* 1 March-30 April 1809.

60) Agnew RAL. Surgeon Leonard Gillespie RN (1755-1842) Revisited. *The Nelson Dispatch*, Spring 2017, 12, pp.614-621.

61) Adkins R and Adkins L. (2006), in *The War for All the Oceans* (2006) ,8, pp.151-153.

62) Hardie DI.(Op.cit.ref 23); 103-05.

63) Hattendorf JB. *The Struggle with France*. (Op.cit.ref 25); 105-06.

64) James W. 'Light Squadrons and Single Ships'. In: *The Naval History of Great Britain, from the Declaration of War by France in 1793 to the Accession George IV*. London: R Bentley & Son 1886; Vol.V, pp 18-22.

65) NA ADM 51/1999.

66) Lavery B. 'Fitting of Ships' (Op.cit.ref 20): *Part III Shipbuilding and Fitting;* p 72.

67) James W. 'Colonial Expeditions - West Indies (1810)' In: *The Naval History of Great Britain, from the Declaration of War by France in 1793 to the Accession of George IV.* London: R Bentley, 1859; Vol.V, p 21.

68) Lyon D. 'The Napoleonic War 1802-1815, 74 gun third rates'. In: *The Sailing Navy List: All the Ships of the Royal Navy - Built, Purchased and Captured, 1688-1855.* London: Conway Maritime Press, 1993: vol.7, p 270. [This records that she was the French D'Hautpoult, built in L'Orient in 1807 and *"Taken in the North Atlantic 17.4.1809"*. (My italics). Presumably the late Mr David Lyon considered the North Atlantic to include the northern Caribbean.]

69) NA ADM 51/1999.

70) NA ADM 37/1905.

71) NA ADM 51/2605.

72) NA ADM 51/2605.

73) Lyon D. (Op.cit.ref.68): xi.

74) Ibid: p 279.

75) Lavery B. 'Fitting of Ships' (Op.cit.ref.40): *Part III - Ship Building and Fitting;* p 70.

76) Parkes EA. (Op.cit.ref.5):15.

77) NA ADM 52/2205.

78) Lyon D. (Op.cit.ref.68): 129-130.

79) Lavery B. 'Fleets'. (Op.cit.ref.40): Part XI; p 250.

80) Parkes EA. (Op.cit.ref.5): 10.

81) Ibid: p 11.

82) Lavery B. 'Officers'. (Op.cit.ref.40): Part IV; p 98.

83) NA ADM 52/2205.

84) Parkes EA. (Op.cit.ref.5): 11.

85) Agnew RAL. 'The Life of Sir John Forbes (1787-1861). Bernard Durnford Publishing, 2002; p 26.

86) NA ADM 51/2954.

87) Lyon D. (Op.cit.ref.68): p 279.

88) Strawson J. 'Peak of Power and a Fatal Blunder' In: *The Duke and the Emperor.* London: Constable, 1994; Chapter 6, p 124.

89) NA ADM 104/30, 509.
90) Lavery B. 'Types of Ship' (OP.cit.ref.40): Part II; pp 43-44.

91) Lyon D. (Op.cit.ref.68): p 39.

92) NA ADM 104/30, 509.

93) Lavery B. 'Shipboard Life'.(Op.cit.ref.40):Part IX; pp 215-16.

94) Hardie DI. 'But the Power is in Others'. (Op.cit.ref.23): chapter 7, pp 113-14.

95) Lavery B. 'Medicine and Health'. (Op.cit.ref.93): p 216.

96) Hardie DI. (Op.cit.ref.94): p 114.

97) Lavery B. 'The Necessities of Life'. Op.cit.ref.93): p 206 - quoting Lloyd C and Coulter JLS. *Medicine and the Navy: 1200-1900.* ref.15; p 325.

98) NA ADM 104/7, 547.

99) Carpenter KJ. 'Scurvy in the British Navy (1700-1772)'. In: *The History of Scurvy and Vitamin C* 1986; Cambridge University Press, Chapter 3, pp 69-72. Table 10.2, p 226.

100) Ibid: p 96.

101) Rocca J & Stolt C-M. 'Royal Naval Physician Sir John Jamison (1776-1844), Scurvy and Sweden's Medico-Surgical Institute'. *Journal of Royal Naval Medical Service* 2002, 88:3, pp 116-126.

102) Carpenter KJ. 'Guinea Pigs and the Discovery of Vitamin C' (1905-1935). (Op.cit.ref.99): Chapter 8, pp 173-197.

103) Lyon D. (Op.cit.ref.68): 244.

104) Lavery B. 'Fleets'. (Op.cit.ref.40): Part XI; p 246.

105) Kennedy L. 'Against Invasion'.(Op.cit.ref.28):Part V, pp 319-21.

106) Lavery B. 'Medicine and Health'. (Op.cit.ref.40): Part IX, p 212.

107) Lavery B. 'The American Navy'. (Op.cit.ref.40):Part XIII; p 286.

108) Ibid: p 288.

109) Lavery B. 'Other Foreign Naval Forces'.(Op.cit.ref.40):Part III; p 291.

110) Lavery B. 'Unrated Ships and Vessels'. (Op.cit.ref.40): Part II; pp 55-56.

111) Lavery B. 'Dockyards and Bases'. (Op.cit.ref.40); Part X; pp 240-244.

112) Strawson J. 'Wellington advances, Napoleon withdraws'. (Op.cit.ref.88): Chapter 9, p 181.

113) James W. (Op. Cit.ref.64):Vol. VI, pp 4-5.

114) Ibid: pp 5-6.

115) Lavery B. 'Amphibious Operations'. (Op. Cit.ref.5): 13-14. page 310

116) Parkes EA. (Op.cit.ref.5): 13-14.

117) Strawson J. 'Wellington advances, Napoleon withdraws'. (Op.cit.ref.88): Chapter 9, p 188.

118) Bernadotte. In: *Chambers Biographical Dictionary.* Gen. Ed. M Magnusson, KBE, Asst. Ed. R. Goring. Fifth edition (1990), Edinburgh: W&R Chambers Ltd., p 145.

119) Lewis M. (Op.cit.ref.44): p 209.

120) Leipzig, Battle of (1813). In: *Chambers Dictionary of World History.* Consultant Ed. Bruce P Lenman, Managing Ed. Katherine Boyd. 1993, Edinburgh: Chambers Harrap Publishers Ltd., p 532.

121) James W. (Op. Cit.ref.111): p 6.

122) Ibid: p 6.

123) Lyon D. (Op. Cit.ref.68): 113-114.

124) Clowes WL. 'Minor Operations 1803-1815'. In: *The Royal Navy. A History from the Earliest Times to the Present.* Vol.V (1900), London: Sampson Low, Marston & Co.,chapter XL: pp 543-44.

125) NA ADM 51/2958 & 37/5184.

126) Lavery B. 'The Admiral's Secretary'. (Op.cit.ref.40): Part XI; p 253.

127) Ibid: p 254.

128) Lloyd C and Coulter JLS. (Op.cit.ref.15): Chapter 6 Hygiene, pp 79-80.

129) Ward JR. 'The British West Indies in the Age of Abolition, 1748-1815'. In: *The Oxford History of the British Empire*. Editor-in-Chief W Roger Louis. Ed. PJ Marshal; Asst.Ed. A Low, 1998; Vol.II The Eighteenth Century, Oxford: Oxford University Press; Chapter 19, p 421.

130) Burns A. 'The War against Napoleon'. In: *History of the British West Indies*, revised second edition 1965. London: Allen and Unwin Ltd. Vol.XIX, p 588.

131) HMC. 'Leith, Sir James (1763-1816)'. (Op.cit.ref.34): p 890.

132) Burns A. (Op.cit.ref.130): p 28.

133) (Op.cit.ref.34): p 890.

134) Kennedy L. (Op.cit.ref.28): Part IV, Champion of the North. pp 249-256.

135) Burns A. (Op.cit.ref.130): p 15.

136) Ibid: p 587.

137) Lloyd C and Coulter JLS. (Op.cit.ref.15): Chapter 13, The Revolution and Napoleonic Wars, 1793-1815, p 173.

138) NA ADM 1/336: letter Q 173.

139) Ibid: Q 185.

140) Ibid: Q 182.

141) Lavery B. 'Relations with the Army'. (Op.cit.ref.40): Part XIV - Tactics: 4 - Amphibious Operations: p 316.

142) HMC. 'Leith, Sir James'. (Op.cit.ref.34): XI, p 890.

143) JKL. 'Durham, Sir Philip Charles Henderson Calderwood (1763-1845)'. (Op.cit.ref.34): VI, p 256.

144) (Op.cit.ref.138): letter Q 183.

145) James W. (Op.cit.ref.111): VI, p 229.

146) JKL. (Op.cit.ref.34): p 258.

147) NA ADM 51/2958.

148) NA ADM 104/30, 509.

149) Ibid: 315.

150) Forbes J. 'A Treatise on the Diseases of the Chest in which they are described in Anatomical Characters, and their Diagnosis established by means of Acoustic instruments'. London: T & G Underwood, 1821.

151) Agnew RAL. 'John Forbes (1787-1861), in memoriam: from Cuttlebrae to Whitchurch' *Journal of Medical Biography1994*; 2: 188-191.

152) NA ADM 1/136: 15777.

153) Ibid: 15777.

154) Porter R. 'Profession, fringe and quackery'. In: *Quacks, Fakers & Charlatans in English Medicine'*. First illustrated paperback edition 2001. Stroud, Glos.: Tempus Publishing Ltd. chapter 8, p 203.

155) 'Virgil's Aeneid': 10, 1.284. In: *The Oxford Dictionary of Quotations.* Revised Fourth Edition. Ed. Angela Partington 1996, Oxford and New York: Oxford University Press: p 714, quotation 7.

Note on references.

From April 2003 the official accreditation of The Public Record Office (PRO) changed to The National Archives (NA); thus the initials NA are used instead of PRO: e.g. ref 52 is NA ADM 51/1642. The ADM references are compiled from entries in the Captain's Log (ADM 51/-) for the respective ships, except for HMS *Cherub* where the Master's Log was used.

The dates of arrival and departure are taken from the Logs and Ship's Muster Books (ADM 37/-).

Basse Terre is in Guadeloupe but Basseterre is in St. Kitts.

REVIEWS

'Robin Agnew has moulded all these many different lives of Sir John Forbes – Royal Physician, translator of Laennec, Victorian polymath and Fellow of the Royal Society (1829) into a fascinating and lively tale set in the nineteenth century...I could not put it down until I had completed it.'

Dr D. Geraint James, Former Consultant Physician to the Royal Navy.

'It is not a long book, but its value lies mainly in the wealth of fascinating detail...concerning medical education, medical advances and practice, naval life and tradition and strategy, the history of the era, and the family of the subject. There are several well-chosen illustrations, and the appendices, notes, suggestions for further reading and bibliography, are excellent.'

Nicholas Coni, Editor, Newsletter of Retired Fellows Society of Medicine, London.